MW00490597

Copyright © January 2008 by Sam J. Sligar

Additional Articles including the Prologue and Epilogue

Copyright © June 2018 by Sam J. Sligar

Published June 2018

by Drawing Conclusions, LLC

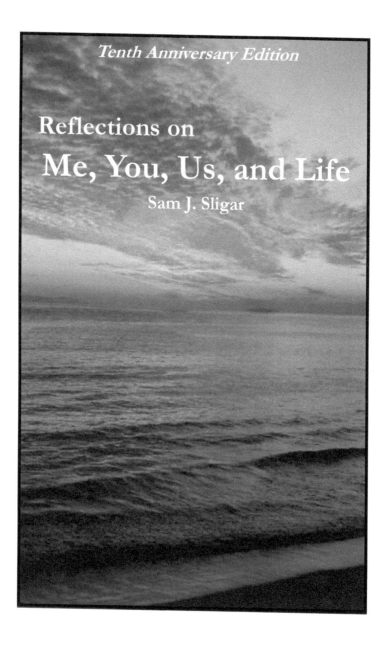

Tenth Anniversary Edition

Reflections on
Me, You, Us, and Life
Sam J. Sligar

To Cathy and Rachel

Introduction

A note that often appeared on my report cards in elementary school was, "Sammy has trouble listening and following directions." I must have learned to listen because, as a counselor, I have made listening my profession for over thirty years. However, I still have problems following directions.

Hundreds of individuals and couples have shared their stories with me. I have listened to them express pain, sorrow, disappointment, great joy and happiness as they struggled to deal with themselves, others and life. For many, it has been a journey that is motivated by pain, endured with courage, propelled by the desire for change, and completed with self/other-awareness and self/other-acceptance. It is still a great privilege to accompany others on such a journey. As a counselor, it is my job to be a "following leader" who is trusted to help guide the way, making sure each person uniquely finds his or her individual way. I see each person as a new "book" to be read and understood, and I have never found a "manuscript" that was not exceedingly interesting.

This book is a collection of articles I have published over the years. They are intended to be short and easily understood, and in this second edition I have added a few articles and edited some to hopefully enhance understanding. In many ways the thoughts and insights here are my "Lessons Learned" from the many journeys I have made with the courageous people who became my "teachers."

Sam

This is the second edition of *Me, You, Us and Life*, and I especially thank Linda Worman of Drawing Conclusions, LLC, for the beautiful work she did in 2008 and again in 2018. I have made some changes in the original and added a few more articles. Much has changed since 2008, but the basic human endeavor of trying to be "Me," caring for and loving "You," while striving to make "Us" work and struggling to live "Life" has not changed so much in the last ten years. However, as impacted mostly by "social media," it has all become more complex, transparent and therefore, even more confusing for many of us.

Table of Contents

Prologue
Lessons Learned Toward a Framework for Understanding and Healing in Relationship

"We must __not__ see any person as an abstraction. Instead, we must see in every person a universe with its own secrets, with its own treasures, with its own sources of anguish, and with some measure of triumph."

Elie Wiesel

Since publishing *Me, You, Us and Life* in 2008, I have discovered there is an underlying theme in my work that defines a relational process I am identifying as perceptual dissonance transforming into perceptual synergy. As you read, I hope you will understand how this process was basic in my personal theory before I ever had a name for it. I hope you will find it helpful to think of this process as a goal in your efforts to communicate and relate as effectively as you possibly can. I am convinced it takes a lifetime of practice and patience, and still we are constantly challenged to really understand one another.

Perceptual Dissonance

I love my work because each person I meet is unique. As Elie Wiesel so beautifully paints with words, "every person a universe of its own." The experiences and relationships that have helped create that "universe" are always remarkably interesting and never finished.

You may be aware of the term "cognitive dissonance" that describes the uncomfortable feeling caused by holding two contradictory ideas simultaneously. For example, cognitive dissonance may be experienced when one supports animal rights and still eats meat. Many studies have been done related to how one can deal optimally with cognitive dissonance in professions like law enforcement and military service where some very difficult decisions need to be made by people who greatly value human life

7

but may be faced with the necessity to take a human life. Cognitive dissonance is sometimes experienced in some very difficult and traumatic decisions, and it is also a very common experience in everyday life. When it occurs, we feel uncomfortable and even hypocritical. Every time I buy something I do not really need but just desire, I experience cognitive dissonance. My parents were survivors of the Great Depression when food, shelter and fuel were treasured, and needless spending was a terrible sinful waste. I think cognitive dissonance is generally good when it helps us to live carefully, and thoughtfully to make good decisions. However, it may not be good when it paralyzes us, and we fail to live as fully and wholly as we were created to be.

Over forty years ago a wise mentor told me more than once that my work as a pastoral counselor and/or a psychotherapist was to help mediate the unending battle between the head and the heart. Finally, I think I can articulate how I understand what he meant. I think my mentor would say that the battle I identify as "cognitive dissonance" is not what he means. The battle of the head and the heart is not one person but the multitude of humanity in a constant state of relationship experiencing the instability of always balancing the "anguish and triumph" of just being human.

There is another kind of dissonance that is far more difficult because it does not happen inside our own minds. It occurs only in the context of relationship. I call this "perceptual dissonance," and it is extremely powerful in a relationship. Neuroscience now confirms that every idea and experience we have is actually processed through the emotional (limbic) part of our brain into the thinking (neocortex) part of our brain. This very complex process creates a "perception." Perceptual dissonance occurs when differing feelings are applied to the same idea or experience.

She says, "What a beautiful sunset!" He says, "It is a nice sunset." She says, "But it is a beautiful sunset. He says, "It is just a sunset." She says, "You never appreciate sunsets. You are not romantic at all." He says, "That is not true. I like sunsets fine." She says, "Well, you never like what I like." Pretty soon the perceptual dissonance will result in a painful argument, and these two people will probably not even remember they were talking about sunsets.

So why is perceptual dissonance such a problem? I believe the problem is that, unlike cognitive dissonance, perceptual dissonance occurs outside of our cognitive awareness. One might say that perceptual dissonance, unlike cognitive dissonance, occurs more in our hearts than in our minds. It occurs mysteriously and nebulously somewhere between us.

To overcome the problem of perceptual dissonance, we first need to be aware and accept that we all have different perceptions because we all have different feelings about our thoughts and experiences. Second, we need to be able to talk about what is in our hearts and listen openly to what is in another person's heart. The second solution can be very challenging because it becomes much more complex when we are beckoned to be aware of our feelings in addition to our thoughts, and actually separate them and ponder how, when and where they came to be. When we can accomplish these solutions, I think perceptual dissonance transforms into perceptual synergy.

Perceptual Synergy

So she says, "What a beautiful sunset!" He says, "It looks like a regular sunset to me." "Really? I think it is beautiful," she says. He asks, "What makes it so beautiful for you?" She answers, "I'm not sure. My mother loved sunsets. Maybe it just reminds me of her." He responds, "I loved your mother very much. She was a wonderful person. I can see why it is so beautiful to you." "Thank you," she replies.

Perceptual dissonance occurs when contradictory feelings are non-consciously applied to the same idea or experience. Since perceptual dissonance only occurs in the context of relationship, and because our feelings are often very different, we frequently have different perceptions. It is important to learn how to transform perceptual dissonance into perceptual synergy.

The first step toward perceptual synergy is to understand there is no such thing as an incorrect perception. This is hard to grasp because we are inclined to automatically assume our perception is the correct perception, and therefore, a differing perception must be incorrect. We fail to account for the reality that a conflicting perception is simply filtered through different and sometimes incompatible feelings. This is why it is often very difficult to discuss religion and politics. Religion and politics are two topics that can carry intense and powerful feelings that greatly influence perceptions.

Creating perceptual synergy is not about creating agreement or endorsement. Perceptual synergy is about creating understanding and respect. In our marriage and family perceptual synergy is essential for relational survival. Therapists are often mocked for our constant interest in feelings. Awareness of feelings is the first step toward perceptual synergy. It is important to realize that feelings can never be right or wrong. Our feelings are attached to all our memories and experiences and therefore are simply true and not right or wrong. When perceptual dissonance becomes conflictual and negating we automatically experience the pain of rejection, because our feelings are unthinkingly being invalidated. We become angry, and we frequently are not consciously aware of why we are hurting or angry. We fail to remember that perception is not just a cognitive process but rather a complex combination of emotion and cognition.

Perceptual synergy is achieved by seeking to understand one's own feelings and understand the feelings of others as they come from the experiences of their life. Because the process is non-conscious, it is incredibly difficult to achieve perceptual synergy. Marriages and families that do achieve an atmosphere of perceptual synergy survive and thrive because there is a pervasive atmosphere of respect, understanding and validation. There is the desire to LEARN!

Me

Do You Really Need to "Explain" Yourself?

Explaining oneself and explaining one's behavior are different. When we are *explaining ourselves* we are probably defending ourselves, and when we are *explaining our behavior* we are educating others about our behavior.

The need to explain ourselves is probably generated by anxiety related to how we think other people are feeling or will feel about us. For example, it is very common for people to have difficulty saying "no" because of the anxiety and fear that the other person will be disappointed, angry, and may not like us. *People pleasers* have a rough time of it because of the fear of being disliked. They frequently have the need to give long explanations so others will not be displeased.

Explaining one's behavior is simply motivated by the need to educate someone about why or how we have behaved. It may even include an apology for our behavior, but not an apology for our existence.

There is absolutely nothing wrong with the need to be a nice person and want the best for other people. However, the idea we can control how others feel and the anxiety this illusion creates is not a good thing. If we are anxious about how someone else feels or may respond, it is a risk to let them freely respond and certainly to discuss it if there are negative feelings or thoughts.

"I don't want to make you angry, but..." This is also a kind of explanation that my intentions are good, so please don't be very angry with me. Ironically the result is that the person will probably be angry no matter what we say because we have tried to control his or her response.

Explaining ourselves to control the response of another person simply does not work. Being clear and presenting our personal feelings without explaining ourselves or the other person works much better.

Playing the Victim Role

"I would like to go but you say we don't have the money."

"Other parents trust their kids, but you won't let me do anything."

"I have to go to work and you get to stay home all day."

"I am stuck in this house all day and you get to go to work."

Being truly victimized by another person or situation is a horrible fate; however, the *victim role* is quite different and very tempting because it can be used to control others when we feel out of control. It is a role we have all played at one time or another.

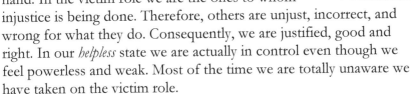

In the victim role we automatically gain an upper hand. In the victim role we are the ones to whom injustice is being done. Therefore, others are unjust, incorrect, and wrong for what they do. Consequently, we are justified, good and right. In our *helpless* state we are actually in control even though we feel powerless and weak. Most of the time we are totally unaware we have taken on the victim role.

In the victim role, we can make others feel pity and guilt when they are angry with us because we are weak and abused. We can even use guilt to make others feel responsible for our unhappiness or our problems.

In the victim role we are not responsible for our reality and thus not to blame if our lives are not as we would like them to be. We have an excuse for not changing, growing, or taking charge of our lives. We get what we want from others by making them feel responsible for our lives and happiness.

Of course, there is a high price to be paid when we play the victim role. The price we pay is the sacrifice of our happiness because our power rests only in our weakness and unhappiness. Time after time true victims of terrible loss and misfortune heroically find contentment and happiness. Unfortunately, when we choose the victim role we also choose to be unhappy.

Achieving Self-Love

I remarked that, "The path to love is having the ability to give it to ourselves and accept it from others." A friend who heard this remarked that he liked the idea, but asked, "How does one achieve self-love?" When I decided to attempt writing an answer to the question I was perplexed with the dilemma of trying to put something so complex into a few sentences, but the more I thought about it I realized there is really only one key deterrent to achieving self-love.

If you think about it, the natural process of human development involves the achievement of self-love. It happens in the context of relationship from the beginning of life and is always moving to a higher level. Observing a toddler or small child one can see how freely he or she interacts with loved ones. You can see clearly that as the interaction is rewarded and enjoyed the self-confidence and self-love of the child is also enhanced. This kind of self-love does not lead to selfishness or self-centeredness, but instead results in a greater capacity to give and receive love in the midst of all the distractions and disappointments life imposes.

The primary deterrent to achieving self-love is shame. Often we think of shame and guilt as being the same. They are not. Guilt makes us feel bad when we make a mistake and hopefully helps us to correct it. Shame makes us feel like we are bad. Shame is the belief that there is something innately wrong and undeserving in us. If we are experiencing shame, we cannot love ourselves, nor can we allow other people to love us. Of all the experiences we have in life, the experience of shame is the greatest threat to the self-love that enables us to truly love others.

The obvious question for another time is— How do I deal with shame?

Dealing with Shame

Best-selling author John Bradshaw describes shame as "the all-pervasive sense that I am flawed and defective as a human being." Psychologist Norman Wright puts it, "Guilt says 'I have made a mistake;' shame says 'I am a mistake.'" Guilt can be frustrating and annoying when it is used for manipulation, or it can be as benign and constructive as Disney's Jiminy Cricket. However, shame is like a virulent cancer that invades the human psyche and can kill the human spirit. How do we know if we suffer from shame?

The most common symptoms are:
All of us have felt these things at one time or another because none

- Hiding and running
- Lack of confidence
- Low self-esteem
- Self-hatred and self–unforgiveness
- Need to justify own existence
- Anger and rage
- Self pity
- Pride, conceit, and judgementalism
- Arrogance
- Difficulty saying "no"
- Compulsions
- Addictions
- Out of touch with one's own feelings
- Perfectionism
- Hopelessness, depression, despair, and feeling tolerated rather than chosen.

of us completely escape shame. However, if any of these symptoms are pervasive, shame may have invaded one's spirit to a greater extent then ever realized.

Once recognized, it is important to understand that we are not born with shame but it has its roots in experiences and relationships. These relationships can be with parents, siblings, friends, peers, teachers, coaches, and even society. The most destructive forms of shame seem to begin in our childhood and lodge themselves deep in our inner psyche only to emerge later in ways that often seem confusing and very frustrating.

Dealing with shame first involves recognizing its existence and discovering its roots. This process helps us to begin the healing because we are starting to take charge by naming the "demons" that torment us. Fighting and controlling these "demons" is a difficult and painful journey, but the culmination of our passage can the freedom to be the person who God truly intended.

Reinventing Yourself

The reasonable man adapts himself to the world; the unreasonable man persists in trying to adapt the world to himself. Therefore all progress depends on the unreasonable man.
George Bernard Shaw

An incredibly unreasonable man, George Bernard Shaw (1856-1950) was a philosopher, satirist, and playwright who loved being at the center of controversy. He also said, "A life spent making mistakes is not only more honorable, but more useful than a life spent doing nothing."

A new phrase for describing personal change is called *reinventing yourself*. It is a new phrase and a very old idea. The need for reinvention is usually motivated by great unhappiness, loss, or other changes that may or may not be in one's control.

Making a major change involves challenging what is reasonable, comfortable, and predictable. It is an open invitation for mistakes and blunders because it means taking a path that is new, unfamiliar and besieged by fear, uncertainty, and indecision. It means the end of complaints and the beginning of actions. It means the end of blaming and the beginning of responsibility. It means acting in spite of fear rather than being paralyzed by the fear of acting. It means anger becomes a motivator and not a terminator. It means happiness becomes a reality and not an idea. **Reinvention is *not* for sissies!**

Anger Management
Dealing with "First Feelings"

When was the last time you expressed anger and regretted it? Anger can be our friend, but when the expression of anger causes undesired and terribly painful results, it can become our enemy. We may be ashamed and even horrified that we did not exercise better control of our anger and our behavior.

Anger Management is a popular topic. There are books, articles, workshops, and even a movie dealing with the subject. Managing anger is not a new topic. It has been a subject of great concern since Cain killed Abel, and it seems little progress has been made since then.

Anger is a feeling that results when we experience something painful. It is important to remember that anger is not the first feeling we experience. Hurt, physical pain, or fear are *first feelings*, and anger can follow almost instantaneously. Managing anger means we must be aware of the *first feelings*, and then we must make choices about how to deal with those feelings. This is not easy because one cannot stop the feeling of anger. Feelings are not chosen; only our reactive behaviors are chosen.

There are many feelings that evoke anger and they are different for every person. What are the painful *first feelings* that make you angry? Rejection, abandonment, helplessness, disappointment, failure, and unimportance are some of the major *first feelings*. Which of these feelings are most powerful for you? The painful experiences of life have a great influence on how angry we feel when we encounter a *first feeling* and how we responded in the past affects how we respond in the present.

Anger management is very difficult, and it may be impossible if we are unaware of the *first feelings*. Identifying our *first feelings* can give us the chance to step back from a situation in which they occur and control our behavior before we regret it.

Good Self Esteem vs. Bad Self Esteem

For many years I have listened to many people struggle with the issue of self esteem. I suppose the struggle comes with the idea that self-esteem is something that can be given and not earned. Self-esteem that is given is based on what others think of us and what we should be. Self esteem that is earned is based on what we think of ourselves and know we can do.

True self-esteem is built upon risk constructed over the foundations of achievement. No child learns to ride a bicycle by listening to lectures on riding; he or she learns by skinning the knees and elbows until the brain (covered by a helmet) discovers the way to stay upright. Neither does the child learn how to walk without accumulating bumps and bruises for his or her trouble. Certainly, encouragement offers some motivation and does contribute to good self-esteem. Good self-esteem is built by discovering what we can do for ourselves, and who we can be for ourselves.

Be suspicious of those who preach the supreme importance of self-esteem. Over-emphasized, it becomes the ultimate goal of parenting, as though a child with self-esteem is automatically good. This child may have merely learned to be what others want him or her to be. All evidence shows this approach merely produces depressed, dysfunctional adults who have no idea what is truly important in life. I view self-esteem as a muscle that needs exercise. Our self-esteem needs to be challenged and worked based on what we can do and who we are. Empty praise for undemonstrated ability is almost always related to the need to be something we are not and therefore produces bad self-esteem. Good self-esteem is built with challenges to meet, high expectations to achieve what we want for ourselves, and being committed to our personal talents and dreams. This produces a person who is toughened to life, who meets with inescapable pitfalls and setbacks, and who possesses the strength to learn from them. This person feels the joy of success that is earned. This person has **good self esteem**.

Change

So there is always in life a place to leave and a new place to find, and in between a zone of hesitation and uncertainty tinged with more or less intense anxiety...There is a past security to be lost before we find a new security. No security lasts, however solid, just or precious...I thought of the trapeze artists, swinging on their trapezes high up under the dome of the circus tent. They must let go of one trapeze just at the right moment to hover for a moment in the void before catching hold of the other trapeze. As you watch, you identify yourself with them, and experience the anxiety of the middle of the way, when they have to let go of their first support and have not yet seized the second.

Paul Tournier, A Place For You, 1968

Change is a constant. We resist it because it always involves some kind of loss, and sometimes it happens whether we want it to or not. The ability to adjust and adapt to change is probably the best measure of our well being as individuals and organizations. Change is a physical, emotional, relational, and spiritual process that we are challenged to achieve every day. Sometimes, however, the changes are very large and very difficult. At those times I think we experience what Paul Tournier describes. We find ourselves moving out of our "comfort zone" and into a place of suspense and uncertainty. The support that comes with the familiar and predictable is taken away and we must remain suspended until the moment is precise to grasp on to a new support.

The time of suspension can be short or long depending on the change we are encountering. It is an anxious time when are aware of our vulnerability. We know that our decisions are exceedingly important as we face our life and future in a way we may not have ever expected. Change can also be an exciting time as we turn to grasp onto a new support that will hopefully take us to a better place. The keys to successful change are found in our hope, faith, patience, communication, resiliency, cooperation, and determination.

When Feelings Become Ideas

A couple days after September 11, 2001 I was making my ritual early morning stop at QuikTrip for coffee. As I prepared my coffee a man dressed in what I identified as traditional Arabian clothing approached to prepare his morning cup of coffee. I was immediately aware of a feeling of fear that translated quickly into an idea that I found appalling and embarrassing. As I thought about this event I was reminded again of what neuro-psychologists are telling us about how we process information. It is now clearly understood that everything we experience enters the **feeling** part of our brain first and then finds its way into the **thinking** part of our brain. In other words, we always feel first and then we think. Feelings are constantly accompanying our experiences and information as they enter the thinking center of our brain, and sometimes these feelings instantly become ideas that we can react to in a variety of ways.

If you see a harmless garden snake, the feeling you have may quickly becomes an idea that results in an action that doesn't do the snake or your garden any good. Sometimes it is important to seriously examine the feelings we have and discern how these feelings are translating into thoughts, judgments, opinions, and actions that have their origins only in our feelings. This can create problems and, as we have seen recently, even terrible acts of aggression. In a relationship between two people it can result in all kinds of conclusions about another person that are very different

from the other person's experience. A harmless frown of confusion can elicit a feeling of rejection that can become an idea that may be very confusing for both people. A nervous laugh can be felt as hurt, which rapidly becomes an idea about being dismissed. Feelings are simply true and not correct or incorrect. On the other hand, ideas based on feelings can be very incorrect. We need to be very careful and aware when our feelings become ideas.

October 1, 2001

Learned Helplessness

In the 1970s Martin Seligman developed the theory of "Learned Helplessness." Seligman discovered his theory by accident while studying classical conditioning of dogs. Seligman expanded his famous theory of "Helplessness" into the realm of human behavior. The premise was very similar in application to people as it was in the animal studies. "Helplessness is a psychological state that frequently results when events are uncontrollable" (Seligman, 1974). Understanding the somewhat boring details of the experiment may help to understand the real power of his conclusions.

- The classic experiment involved two groups of dogs, Group A and Group B. Both groups received moderate electric shocks while strapped into a hammock.

- Group A dogs could turn the shock off by pushing a panel with their noses. They could do this anytime after the shock began.

- Each dog in Group B was "yoked" to a dog in Group A which meant that whenever the Group A dog was shocked, so was the corresponding Group B dog, and whenever the Group A dog turned off its shock, the shock was also turned off for the corresponding Group B dog. The dogs in the two groups received exactly the same number of shocks and for the same duration at the same time, putting Group B dogs in a situation where they had no power to control their environment. For Group B dogs, the shocks seemed inescapable, even though the actual physical punishment was identical.

- The crux of the experiment was learning. The key question was, in a new situation where the dogs can actually help themselves, will the dogs who were able to exercise control over their circumstances learn differently compared to dogs who simply had to endure the shocks?

- The dogs from both groups were put in a "shuttle box' and then presented with a conditioned stimulus (e.g. bell and light) 10 seconds before the floor becomes electrified. The shuttle box has a barrier the dog could jump over to the other side which was not electrified. Learning was quantified by measuring the number of seconds it took for the dog to jump over in a period of ten or so trials. If the dog jumped within 10 seconds of hearing the bell, it avoided the shock altogether. If it failed to jump after 60 seconds of shocking, the electricity was turned off. To avoid the shock, all the dog had to do was jump over the barrier.

- Group A dogs learned quickly to avoid the shock.
- Sadly, the Group B dogs, the ones who had experienced inescapable shock in the hammock, reacted passively. They did not look for an escape. Seligman wrote, "They laid down, whined quietly, and simply took whatever shocks were delivered. They neither avoided nor escaped; they just gave up trying." Even after repeated trials, the Group B dogs never discovered that they could avoid the shock simply by jumping over the hurdle. (These experiments conducted on animals and humans in the early years of behavioral psychological are today judged to be inhumane and illegal.)

What happened after the experiment was not scientifically documented, but I believe is very important knowledge. Seligman reported that after seeing what happened to these poor dogs, he and his colleagues were mortified by what had happened to them, "We dragged those poor, reluctant animals back and forth across the shuttle box over the barrier and back again at least two hundred times in two days until they began to move under their own steam and came to see that their own actions worked. Once

they did, the cure was one hundred percent reliable and permanent."

The very important conclusion was "A dog (or presumably, a person) can be 'immunized' against learned helplessness in a particular situation, and dogs who learned that responding matters, **never** acquired that particular learned helplessness again."

When life overwhelms us with loss and/or problems to be solved, we can learn helplessness without ever knowing what is happening to us. We begin to feel so trapped we can't even see obvious solutions when they are presented to us. In our depression we do not realize we have actually learned to be helpless and passive. The darkness is just replaced by more darkness.

Having some degree of control and not feeling completely helpless greatly improves performance, especially for those who are depressed and feel an all-around lack of control. This supports the idea that identifying and experiencing the areas of life one can control may help considerably in dealing with the depression and helplessness resulting from the areas one cannot control. This is very good news for dealing with learned helplessness. However, this is not the first step.

I believe overcoming learned helplessness begins with acknowledging or confessing that the learning has actually occurred. This is an enormous step because the awareness actually begins to loosen the shackles of the ideas, pain, and fears that bind us. Taking this responsibility for learning helplessness confronts us with the arduous task of unlearning the helplessness that is fed and nourished by depression. After taking the steps of awareness and responsibility, it should be noted that faith, hope, and love (relationship) are powerful "medications" for unlearning helplessness and fighting depression. It takes the help of those who understand and patiently help us "across those barriers" until we unlearn our helplessness and are empowered to care for ourselves.

Defining Maturity

"My husband is so immature," she says. "He needs to grow up."

What do we mean when we judge another person pronouncing they are immature? If we mean that the other person is acting like a child, what is problematic about that? Children can be the most loving creatures on earth, so why is immaturity necessarily a problem?

I believe maturation is a process that is reflected in how we relate to others and that very few people actually reach full maturity. I think maturity is reflected in the value that "I am important **and** you are important." Immaturity is reflected in the de-value that says, "I am important and you **are not** important," or "I am **not** important and you **are** important."

"Love your neighbor as (not more and not less than) yourself." If you think about it, this is incredibly difficult to accomplish in a family, much less a neighborhood, town, state, country, or world. If humanity ever reached that level of maturity, what would happen? I suppose this world would look a lot more like the Kingdom of God than it does right now.

Since global maturity seems a long way off, you and I are probably best served by striving to build on our own maturity, one step at a time, within our own families and communities.

I believe it is easier to be mature when there is harmony in our relationships. I have discovered that our level of immaturity is most exposed for measurement when we are arguing or disagreeing with each other. This is when we are most vulnerable to losing track of the importance of others or ourselves. For example, if you believe that arguing means winning or losing, then you probably have some maturing to do. If arguing results in someone feeling unimportant, then both people have some maturing to do. The degree of winning, losing and unimportance that is experienced in an argument is a good measure of the degree of maturity or immaturity of the participants. If you and I use this measure, how mature are we? Always remember that we should only measure our **own** level of maturity. If we measure and judge other people, we are only revealing our immaturity.

Introduction to a Monster

"Let me introduce myself to you!" I am a Monster, and I am not far from you all the time. I am dangerous and can even kill. My name is "Depression." I take pleasure in being a universal malady of the human spirit that respects no boundaries of gender, geography, culture, religion, race, class, or wealth. Let me further educate you about me.

I am dark without form or shape. Sometimes I am lucky enough to actually live inside of you and ravage your mind and spirit at whatever time I choose. Whenever you are so unfortunate, and I am so fortunate to actually reside in the inner recesses of your being, your stupid so-called professionals refer to me as "Clinical Depression." I don't know what "clinical" really means, but I know that I like it because it is absolutely the best of all worlds for me. They say that medications combined with therapy can attack me. Don't believe a word they say. They are all greedy quacks.

Unfortunately, it is rare that I am so lucky as to actually reside on the inside. Therefore, I contentedly lurk in the shadows all around you until I am able to infect you. I am so skillful in my ability you don't even recognize me. I am like a leech that attaches and quietly sucks your life's blood (your spirit) out of you. When you have been successfully infected, you are completely unaware of my presence. I have often said that I am a "monster that feeds on myself." The feelings and thoughts I generate are actually my nourishment. I may be two feet tall or two hundred feet tall depending on how much food I can generate from your anxieties, fears, frustration, helplessness, and hopelessness. I am insidious as I wait for an opening into your body, mind, and spirit. If you recognize me, I immediately inform you that if you weren't so weak, I wouldn't be here. Even to say, "I am depressed" is a serious threat to my existence. If you say these words, I will make you feel like the confession of your pain is an admission of your weakness and lack of courage. I will make you feel worthless and embarrassed that you have let me take control.

There is one "food" that I cannot exist without. I must be fed by your loneliness, or I will die. I will use hopelessness to prevent you from reaching out and connecting with another human being. I love to wake you up at 3:00 in the morning when you are the most alone. However, you will feel lonely even in a crowded room, as I thrive on your isolation and misery. That you know how to kill me does not concern me, because when I take control, you will forget all you have read here, and **I will thrive!**

How Important are You?

From the day we are born till the day we die, we may struggle to understand the "what," "where," "when," and "how to" of our importance to others. From the earliest age we strive to be important and special to those we love. The first moment comes when we perceive the face of our mother, and, as our vision stabilizes, we see and feel love and adoration for the first time. It "explodes" in our tiny brains giving us a feeling of profound security that is permanently imprinted. When we lose it, we experience terror that is expressed in screams that bring us the comfort we feel in our mother's arms. Gradually we internalize the trust that is the building block for giving ourselves the necessary feeling of safety and security when we need to navigate the "storms" of life. In the next stages, at about age three, we become explorers who can leave the safety of our mother's arms until anxiety overcomes and we run back to the arms of love and reassurance. We feel loved and important.

There are many more developmental bridges we have to cross in our families, our friendships, our schools, our community. It is not an easy journey to build the confidence, self-worth, and feeling of importance we need to finally be true to ourselves. If, for some reason, we don't get across those bridges successfully we struggle to figure out what will give us the importance we need and relieve the pain of not feeling valued and important. At this point, we may begin a lifetime of trying to manufacture that importance we failed to internalize in our childhood. There are many paths we may take to find the importance we need. We may seek the declaration of our importance by rebelling against authority or by controlling others and become a bully. It may manifest itself in how we dress, the grades we make, the sports we excel in, the career we choose, the money we make, the kind of person we marry, the car we drive, and even the accomplishments of our children. However, these things we think make us important never quite make it happen the way we non-consciously intended. It does not fill the void we feel. The emptiness is filled with superficial things and ideas that do not give back love. We feel and believe that we are not good enough and that what others have is better and would make us feel good and important if we had what they have. This is envy, and it "eats our souls."

It is often in our desperation to feel worthwhile and important that we become "human-doings," and we lose track of what it means to be "human-beings." Our real importance is not found in how we perform and what we have. It is only in the context of relationship that we experience our real importance. When we allow ourselves to become vulnerable and form nurturing, safe relationships with others, we become far more important than we dreamed we could be. It is not based on what we do but on who we are. It is based on the love and understanding we give and the love and understanding we allow others to give us. We perceive our importance most clearly when we are vulnerable and realize how much others really do care about us. It is those times we feel truly understood and accepted "warts and all." Then we **know** we are important.

The Denial of the Negative

In a restaurant recently, my wife and I overheard a middle-aged couple at the next table. They were clearly in the early stages of their relationship and were establishing the groundwork by explaining some important aspects of their personalities. Since they were so preoccupied with their efforts to establish their identities with one another, they were unaware most people nearby could hear the entire conversation. After they left, my wife asked me if I thought there was something odd about the couple's efforts to introduce themselves to one another. It suddenly occurred to me that they were not concerned about telling one another about who they were, but almost exclusively defined themselves to each other by who they were not. "You don't have to worry about that with me," she would assure him. "I will never do that," he would insist.

It seemed rather sad that this was how two people defined themselves, but I wonder if we too often tend to define ourselves by the denial of the negative rather than the affirmation of the positive. Listen how others tell you about themselves. Take a close look at the many forms we fill out and the number of times we must deny the negative. It is sad that the "negative" has so much power.

Listening to Pain

If you break your leg, you will feel intense pain. The pain is telling you there is something very wrong with your leg, and the pain is so strong you do not attempt to use the leg, which of course would cause further damage to the leg. If you went to the emergency room and the physician just treated the symptom of pain, he or she would simply use drugs to make the pain go away and send you home. Of course, that would be ridiculous because everyone knows the physician would have to treat the cause of the pain and provide an environment for the bone to heal. You will instead go home with your leg in a cast and maybe with some pain medication to help while your leg begins the complex process of healing itself.

Emotional and psychological pains are sometimes very similar to physical pain because the pain is telling us that something is wrong and needs attention. However, many times we do not listen to emotional pain and simply treat the symptom thus ignoring what is causing the hurt. These are times when we also become angry at the cause of the pain. At these times, it would be like leaving the emergency room with a broken leg, a lot of painkillers and no cast. Anger may be a "painkiller" but it is NOT a "cast."

Emotional pain can come in different forms, like sadness, fear and anger. If you or someone else has one of these feelings, it is a sign that something is wrong. Whether the pain is very small or very large, we often try to ignore the feelings and just make them go away. This approach can be very inadequate because we fail to provide the environment for healing.

Emotional healing, like physical healing, is an extraordinarily complex process. The environment for emotional healing is usually found in a relationship that comprehends the complexity and "blood, sweat and tears" of emotional healing. Emotional healing occurs when we able to trust another person to listen and truly try to understand. It is an embracing environment that holds and accepts the feelings, much like the cast holds the leg in a safe place while it heals. Hopefully our family and friends are the primary environments for our emotional healing, but sometimes more is needed to heal wounds that are hard to understand, and may also be personal and private. That is when trusted professional help may be a good solution.

Listening to pain is always important. Turning a deaf ear really doesn't work and can cause even worse damage and greater pain. The "leg" never really heals as it should.

Looking for Angels

When a person seeks counseling it is usually because they have encountered personal or relational problems they cannot resolve. A part of the process of counseling is to discover how that person has learned to relate and cope with problems throughout their life because those ways may not be working well.

During our childhood we acquire basic assumptions about our relationships and ourselves. From our childhood we may acquire the basic assumption that we can generally trust other people and depend on them. Because of our childhood experiences we may also assume that we are good, interesting, and worthwhile, and we seek to see others as good, interesting, and worthwhile. Hopefully we assume the world is generally a good and safe place to be even though it can be very bad and unsafe at times.

Unfortunately, many childhood experiences do not result in positive and constructive assumptions. Whenever I discover that someone has suffered a childhood which has resulted in assumptions that they are not good, interesting, and worthwhile, I want to know who taught them these assumptions and how. More importantly, however, I also know that somewhere they received good messages because those messages are the ones that have caused them to ask questions and to seek counseling. It is important to find out who gave them the good messages because that is the source of their strength. Those people are their "angels." It can be anyone – parent, sibling, grandparent, aunt, uncle, cousin, neighbor, minister, coach, teacher, and many others.

Hopefully you have many angels from your childhood, but if not, think about who really made a difference for you and helped you to think better of yourself and gave you strength, and confidence, and love. They are your angels. Be thankful for them because they gave you a precious gift. They are your "Angels!"

I Think, Therefore I Am
or is it I feel, therefore I am?

In the sixteenth century René Descartes applied mathematical method to philosophy and became one the founder's of modern philosophy. Descartes concluded, "I think, therefore I am." This conclusion has generally been accepted as truth particularly in the scientific and medical community. However, recent brain studies suggest, in terms of brain structure, emotion has a greater position of influence than cognition. The limbic brain, which contains the emotional center of the brain, actually is the first to receive all incoming information and has more neural projections than the neocortex, the thinking part of the brain. The limbic brain is also more highly developed than the neocortex and, unlike the neocortex, can activate every physiological response without consulting the *thinking brain*.

The scientific and medical community is finally joining the community of psychology and religion who have long known that people need to access the deeper levels of their being and pay attention to what we feel as well as what we think. As we enter the twenty-first century, we are in agreement that it is the combination of feeling and thinking that actually makes us what God intended us to be. The truth, as we now understand it is, "I feel **and** think, therefore I am."

The Double Bind of Fear

"Watch out!" **"Don't touch that! Don't run!"** **"Don't, don't, don't... or you'll get hurt."** We are taught at a very young age to be afraid and that not learning to listen to fear will result in physical pain or worse. Of course, the motive is to protect but then a few years later our peers may declare, **"Don't be afraid."** **"Only sissies are afraid."** The double bind is complete. Fear is good, and fear is bad.

So is it any wonder that we grow up feeling very confused about fear. It is a feeling that protects but also can humiliate us. The dysfunctional solution is to declare we are never afraid. Then we are pushed too far with, **"I dare you!"** We do something immensely stupid just to show we are not afraid. We may have a broken bone, but we have proven we are **not** afraid.

I think it is very important to learn at an early age that fear is a very essential and important feeling. I believe is important to teach children about the double bind of fear. It is a feeling that we use constantly to make judgments related to our safety and wellbeing. As physical pain occurs to keep us from wounding ourselves, fear helps us to perceive, evaluate and engage almost all of our activities of daily living. We each have to struggle to balance our use of fear because the "bad" side of fear can paralyze us so that we do not use our knowledge of the double bind of fear to optimize our safety even when we take risks that enable us to live fully. Fear should be taught as a positive and essential feeling that we use to make ourselves safe and happy, and it is a negative when it keeps us from enjoying life and engaging in the risks that make life good. Fear is a double bind that helps us live life intentionally and judiciously.

Emotional Reality vs. Rational Reality

"Why are you so late? Why didn't you call? I called you four times!"

She responds, "This is so ridiculous. You knew exactly where I went, and I was not gone that long. I forgot my cell. Is that a crime? You do this all the time! You are so controlling!"

Rational Reality
When Jim was three years old his father was killed in a car accident. Jim has no memory of this. It is just part of his story. Jim grew up in a great relationship with his step-father. It is real.

Emotional Reality
There is a preverbal part of Jim's memory that remembers his father's death. It is entirely an emotional memory. It is real.

Rational Reality
Jim actually knows his wife tries to let him know where she is and calls when she can. He can't understand why he gets so angry when she doesn't call. This is real.

Emotional Reality
Ann becomes very angry when Jim acts so unreasonably controlling and sometimes forgets her cell phone on purpose just to get back at him. This is real.

The collision of the emotional realties and rational realities goes on for years until they get completely fed up with it and seek some counseling.

When I hear Jim's story I ask him if he remembers or has been told how he reacted when his father died. He does not. Fortunately his mother is living and he can ask her. He learns that he became very clingy after his father died. He started sucking his thumb again and wanted a bottle. He screamed and cried in terror whenever his mother left and it took several months until she could leave him with anyone else or even to get him to sleep by himself.

Jim brings this story to our session. I ask Jim how he feels as he retells the story his mother told him. He says he feels very sad. Ann, who is the mother of two, quietly weeps.

The emotional realities and rational realities begin to take on a new framework. The intensity of Jim's feelings is reduced, and Ann now rarely forgets her cell phone.

Emotional realities and rational realities are always both "real." Neither should be ignored, disrespected, or go unexplored when they are in conflict.

Fear of the Unknown

"Fear of the unknown" is a common expression, but when one really thinks about it, "fear of the unknown" does not make sense. It is a puzzling that we actually assume we know anything about the unknown. The reality is that we absolutely know nothing about the next second, minute, hour, day or year of our existence. We all know that at any moment our lives can be completely altered in a very wonderful or an incredibly terrible fashion. Many of us have experienced this personally and everyday we hear about people whose lives are spun into a completely different orbit of wonderful happiness or excruciating pain.

In spite of the fact that we live our lives in a constant state of unknowing, we go to bed every night assuming we will get up the next morning and proceed with our daily routine. We get into our cars and drive into the perilous paths of rush hour traffic believing we will eventually arrive at our destination. We distract ourselves calling a family member or friend presuming they are fine, even if they do not answer our call. We also assume we will not become a "statistic," thus validating the foolishness of using a cell phone in rush hour traffic.

We are NOT afraid of the unknown. We fearlessly face the unknown with every breath because of what we "think" we know.

We are also "afraid" of the unknown because of what we "think" we know. This can certainly keep us safe when we use our fear to carefully evaluate our decisions, and therefore, tread into the unknown being informed and cautious. This helps us make better personal, social, relational and financial decisions.

Fear of what we "think" we know can also plague us with ideas or phobias about consequences and outcomes that may or may not be realistic. Fearful thoughts of the unknown can cause us to fear and even avoid many activities.

I often remind myself that an elevator will not plunge to the ground just because I enter, or that a plane will crash just because I am a passenger. However, a recent tragic airline accident could create uncertainty. I may become more anxious and apprehensive about what I "think" I know about flying. These feelings of anxiety and fear could influence me so that I could become cynical and pessimistic about flying. The negativity could feed on itself producing thoughts of doom, and I could become "grounded." I would lose the healthy balance of optimistic thinking and pessimistic thinking that facilitates the best possible outcome. Transportation!

Fear of what we "think" about the unknown is influenced by many circumstances. During the good times the "glass is always half full," and we assume good things. During the bad times the "glass is always half empty," and we assume bad things. Fortunately and unfortunately, our assumptions can become "self-fulfilling prophesies." It can mean the difference between being "grounded" and "flying.

Worry Wart!

If you have never heard these words before, then you need not read any further. If you have heard these words, I invite you to join the rest of us "Worry Warts," and be a part of our fellowship. We are also told that we are overprotective and unrealistic. On the contrary, we believe we are perfectly justified, and we are offended to be dismissed with a diagnosis of "Worry Wart."

Usually we hear these indictments of our caring from the people we care for the most, such our children, our spouses, and now those in the "Sandwich Generation" are actually hearing it from elderly parents, who are perceived as needing more protection than the parents think they need. A "Worry Wart's" job is never done."

Our adult daughter, who lived the mountains of Virginia a few years ago, was diagnosed with Lyme Disease. I was like a "Worry Wart on Crack." I admit that I was "over the top" for the situation. I was learning everything I could from the internet, which can scare a "Worry Wart" to death. Yes, I called too many times, sent too many texts and too much information. Of course, she took care of herself and recovered nicely. I am lucky she was understanding, but I also needed to know there are limits and "stop" really does mean, "Stop!" She now refers to that time as, "OSama Care," for those of you who remember "Obama Care."

I would like to call a truce between all the "Worry Warts" and their "victims." I think it is time for us to find some better ways of communicating so that we are heard and not dismissed. A "truce" means that both sides need to understand and change. We "Worry Warts" need to accept the fact that we can be a real pain in the backside. We can overwhelm others with our need to help, to fix, to protect, to advise etc. The trick to changing this is to understand that we are coming out of our fear and anxiety, which can easily hijack our brains and our communication. It is imperative both sides understand this process because the response to the worrier is usually anger and defensiveness.

We need to challenge the assumptions that emerge after years of dealing with a "worry wart." It gets to the point that a simple question like, "Did you remember your coat?" is experienced as just the beginning of the "worry wart" attack. The response probably will be, "Of course I remembered my coat. Stop nagging me!" The worrier responds, "I was just asking a question." Usually this is followed by an irritated sigh and silence. On the other hand, it may escalate. This depends on the history and the intensity of the anger. It can get really ugly. I have not met one couple who are content being stuck in the angry cycle that worrying can create.

It is very difficult in any relationship to challenge our assumptions and choose to pursue a path of really talking and listening to how both people are feeling. This also may mean exploring the root of some of our fears and anxieties, so the other person understands both our rational and our emotional realities. We worriers need to understand that our emotional realities can be overwhelming to the other person and there does need to be limits that both people understand and accept. This is so much easier said than done, but I know for sure it is not impossible if both people really want to stop.

The "Overreacting Diagnosis"

What does it mean when someone makes a "diagnosis" that you are "overreacting?" How do you feel? The diagnosis of overreacting usually means that your reaction is unreasonable, invalid and even ridiculous resulting in the feeling that you are also unreasonable, invalid and ridiculous. Now you are angry and defensive.

It is confusing when I hear the diagnosis of overreacting. It may be clear there is a strong emotional reaction present, and it may also be clear that the emotional reaction seems out of proportion to the content and even the tone of the discussion. The reaction seems to be coming out of somewhere that is not obvious, and the recipient dismisses it as an overreaction. Furthermore, the person who is reacting cannot understand why he or she is not understood and is forced into an angry and defensive position.

Life gives us thousands of experiences in hundreds of relationships that all serve to inform how we feel about ourselves and how we react. For example, if a person has experienced life in a way that has resulted in a fear of disapproval, he or she may react with pain and feel wounded if it is perceived someone dislikes something he or she has done. The wounded person may become very upset and attack the one who has inflicted the pain of disapproval. The assailant may then become defensive and dismiss the wounded one as overreacting. Actually, the reaction is in direct proportion to the pain that is experienced when disapproval is perceived whether it was intended or not.

Since the "Overreacting Diagnosis" will likely often be communicated, the best advice I can give is to recognize that whenever you are diagnosed as overreacting, try to resist going into the natural defensive position, and ask yourself, "What is it that either I or this other person does not understand about why I am having such a strong reaction?" A useful response might be, "I am reacting to something that is real and valid to me, and I am not sure you or I know why I feel such a strong reaction. I think I need to stop and figure this out."

It would be wonderful if we could recognize and be in charge of our feelings as effectively as I just described, but we are not. My hope, however, is that as a result of reading this, you will think differently whenever you give or hear the "Overacting Diagnosis."

You

Sarcasm is one of the most popular forms of comedy. From George Burns, Jackie Gleason, and Don Rickles to George Carlin, Jerry Seinfeld, Lewis Black, and Ellen Degeneres, the art of "Sarcasm" has made it incredibly funny when one person uses exaggeration to diminish the validity and credibility of another. It works on the stage, the movie theater, and on television, but it is not so funny in families, marriage, and in actual relationships. For more than forty years in the movies and television we enjoyed the hilarious violence of The Three Stooges. In real life this kind of violence is not entertaining, except for pathetic bullies.

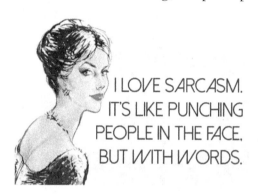

I LOVE SARCASM. IT'S LIKE PUNCHING PEOPLE IN THE FACE. BUT WITH WORDS.

Sarcasm is actually a form of *relational violence* that can cause excruciating pain. My father often used sarcasm, and whenever we approached a bridge with a weight bearing limit of three or four tons, he would remark that my mother needed to get out of the car and walk across so the car would not exceed the limit. Of course, no one ever challenged this cruel reference to her weight problem and, because we lived in the country, we crossed many bridges.

Sarcasm is confusing because at the same time a humorous message is delivered, so is a painful one. It grows even more confusing and painful because the one who is being sarcastic can defend his or her actions by saying, "I was just kidding," and then follow that with, "Can't you take a joke?" The double bind is complete. Not only are you in pain from the message, now you are a weak and fragile person because you can't take a joke. You are demoralized, angry, and powerless.

In the *sarcasm arena* of some families, there is often a very unfair inequality in which parents are allowed to be sarcastic with their children without apology, but children are considered appallingly disrespectful when they imitate the sarcasm and bestow it upon their parents. Respect should always be a two-way street in families, and perhaps all relationships. Using sarcasm to express our anger or disappointment inevitability leads to someone feeling disrespected and diminished. This is really not the way we want the people we love to feel, but it unfortunately happens too often.

It is embarrassing to be confronted with the pain we might inflict with our sarcasm, and it requires a lot of strength to face our embarrassment and express our feelings directly and honestly. Saying, "I am angry with you" hurts others much less than expressing anger through sarcasm.

I think it is best to allow the great artists to practice the "Art of Sarcasm" and leave sarcasm out of our real relationships.

What Does Your Mirror Reflect?

When an infant is able to focus on its mother's face, she is the infant's first **human mirror.** Hopefully, the reflection the infant sees is one of joy, welcoming him or her into this world. This initial reflection is incredibly important for the infant because it is their first experience of love and acceptance. It is this continued love and acceptance that sets the stage for self-acceptance and love that later becomes the ability to give love and acceptance to others.

It is easy for us to see how others are mirrors for us. If we see a look of anger or disappointment in another person's face, we use that reflection to make decisions about how we feel about ourselves. We are all aware of how positive we feel when someone smiles and seems to like us, and if our world of mirrors has been good enough, we can trust that we are lovable and acceptable.

We are much more aware of the mirrors we use than the fact that we are also a mirror that is used by others. What do you reflect in your mirror? What do people see when they use you for a mirror? For the people we love, we are one of their most important mirrors. What does your spouse see when you come together after a day apart? What reflection do you give your child or children? Do they know you are happy with them and find them interesting?

Do you ever consider what kind of reflection you want to give people in general? You are always a mirror to be used by others. When you encounter other people in everyday life, what reflection do you want to give them? What kind of reflection do you give to the people who wait on you in a store or restaurant? Do you give the reflection you want to project, or are you not sure? How often do you smile (or do you even know)? What do the people at your work see in the mirror you provide?

I know that it is very easy for me to forget that I am a mirror and that I have unlimited opportunities to provide reflections which can help people see themselves and feel their importance. If you and I try to consciously be good mirrors, I think the results could be very interesting and very positive.

I Love You. Therefore, You Owe Me

There is a conflict in relationships I have observed numerous times. I describe this conflict as a struggle with the feeling and belief that being loved is contingent on fulfilling conditions or obligations. Even though First Corinthians 13 assures us that, "Love does not insist on its own way," I find that many people have been conditioned to believe, "if you love me, then I owe you." This belief begins with the message, "I love you. Therefore, you owe me." I believe this message is not one that most parents would ever want to give their children, however, many do. It begins in the early years of development. It is the spoken and/or unspoken message generally that, "I will love you as long as you do not disappoint me and will reject you if you do." As this message is internalized, the child grows into adulthood concluding that in a relationship, "If you love me, then I owe you." This conclusion causes a person to be wary of love and not to trust that they could be loved simply for themselves. They are loved only for what they can do or perform. They are also often confused when the good things they do and accomplish do not result in the love they want. They are never good enough.

It can be very painful to live within the paradigm that love is something to be earned. In this paradigm it also seems the words are rarely or never spoken aloud. In a "love by works" relationship a child usually gauges love by the absence of negative feedback and not the presence of positive words of affirmation. Some children will spend their whole childhood trying to please and earn love. Others may take a different path and act out in anger and rebellion. Whatever the response, the result is an "empty hole" that is never filled; not by great works and wonderful performances, and certainly not by more anger and rebellion.

Unfortunately, after growing up in the "love by works" world no one can give us enough love to fill the hole. We must give it to ourselves and eventually learn to believe it and receive it from others. This is very difficult when we have convinced ourselves that love can only be earned. The path to love is paved carefully with the ability to give love to ourselves and, most importantly, the vulnerability to accept it from others we believe we can trust.

Constructive Criticism

Someone says to you, "I would like to give you some constructive criticism." What is your first response? Is it, "Wow! I am really looking forward to hearing this!" or is it, "Ouch!"?

Constructive criticism is actually an oxymoron that gives a confusing positive and negative message simultaneously. It is the pain of the negative that is stimulated and not the pleasure of the positive. For this reason, I believe that constructive criticism cannot be given; it can only be received.

Receiving criticism and transforming it into something constructive is a process we must do for ourselves. The power to transform criticism into constructive criticism is greatly dependent on the degree to which we have been taught self-respect and have experienced feeling good about ourselves. If we grow up in a very critical environment that diminishes our self-esteem and leaves us feeling ashamed, our confidence in our power to transform criticism is greatly weakened. We may not even realize that we have the power to transform criticism.

In its most toxic form, criticism is delivered with a tone and words that shame and condemn. Criticism can strike us with piercing pain that leaves us depleted and demoralized. If we are already critical of ourselves, even the most benign criticism can cause significant pain. Regardless of how criticism is given, it is ultimately in our power to process it and make it into something constructive rather than destructive.

Making a criticism constructive is accomplished by cognitively setting aside the negative feelings and examining the content of the message. Are there suggestions or observations that make sense and offer me a different way of doing what I am doing? Do

I need more information about what the person is telling me, and can I hear the information without being defensive? Even if I don't like what I am hearing, do I trust this person's motive for giving me criticism?

If we can pursue criticism with the desire to learn and possibly change and grow, then we can make it constructive. However, we must learn to listen carefully to both the feelings and the content of a criticism. If we determine that the motive is simply to hurt us, then it is really about the one delivering the message and not about us.

It is important to remember that we cannot really give constructive criticism, and we need to appreciate the difficult transformation process others can have even when our suggestions or critiques are caring and well intentioned.

Double Messages

Virginia Satir was a leader in the field of family therapy and made many contributions to understanding how families function and why they have so much trouble sometimes. One concept she explored was the effect of the *double message*. Virginia Satir said, "Double messages are crazy making."

Anyone who has experienced a double message knows how crazy it can make one feel. It is most often received in a sentence that contains the word *but*. I think you look very nice today, but…."

Double messages can come in different containers. Both words and actions can deliver double messages. If I say I am glad to see you, but my actions basically ignore you, then you receive a double message and you feel confused and even crazy if you receive these kinds of messages over a long period of time.

- **Chronic exposure to double messages leads to a profound confusion about what is real and not real.**
  This can result in feelings of anxiety, uncertainty, insecurity and paralysis when it comes to decision-making. Double messages make it impossible to trust.
  "I love you, but don't bother me."
  "I will be there for you…. next time."
  "I am proud of you but I hope you do better the next time."
  Double messages can make us feel guilty.
  "Go have a wonderful time and don't worry about leaving me here all alone."

- **Over a long period of time double messages can create a very troubled and unhappy person.**
  Double messages can occur in a marriage, a family, a job, and a community. It would be wise to examine how we all give and receive double messages, and explore how we can achieve greater consistency.

People Boxes

In the world of psychology and psychotherapy there is a manual called the *Diagnostic and Statistical Manual of Mental Disorders (DSM)*. This manual is intended to be used to connect the world of psychiatry and psychology with the world of medical diagnosis and particularly medical insurance.

Students are generally fascinated by the diagnostic manual because it helps to alleviate the anxiety accompanying the overwhelming task of understanding human behavior. It also offers a tempting illusion — that people can be placed in categories and *boxes* which then define how they will be treated and healed. In reality, these attempts generally result in little healing for the patient and much frustration for the clinician.

We try to place people in boxes in many ways. We are constantly attempting to explain behavior by explaining the person. "He never smiles because he is a grump." "He doesn't come to church because he is not a Christian." "She doesn't speak to me because she is stuck up." "He is tired because he is a workaholic." We use some other more profane diagnoses too, but none of them serve us very well except to keep us isolated and ignorant.

Any *People Box* we create is actually a flimsy container that cannot sustain the forces of curiosity and understanding. This is true even for the personal boxes we create to protect ourselves. The more one knows about a person the more difficult it is for that person to remain in the box. The closer one gets to another person and the more one discovers about that person, the bigger he or she becomes. Soon there is not a box that even begins to fit. In fact, the *People Box* is no longer needed or helpful.

Ignorance and indifference are the only ways to build and sustain a *People Box*. Unfortunately, we live in a world where there is an abundance of both. Fortunately it is a world where there is also an abundance of curiosity and understanding.

48

Setting the Tone

I have been doing counseling for over thirty years, and I hear couples debate what a *tone of voice* means at least ten times a week. That adds up to over ten thousand times I have heard couples discuss the confusion and disagreement about whether a certain tone exists and what message it is sending.

It all begins very early as we hear our parent say, "Don't use that tone with me young man (or young lady)!" Our look of confusion pleads our innocence but we are not believed. We may even go through our lives protesting the messages our tones send, and at the same time being very sensitive to the tones we hear and the messages they give us. The truth is that there is a message conveyed by intonation with every verbal communication we deliver, and the message of our tone can be very different from the content of the verbal message thus creating a double message. Innumerable times I have heard, "Why are you so angry? I said I would do it." Or I have heard, "I was just telling you the facts. Why are you so defensive?"

So how does one correct the problem of setting a tone that delivers a double message? One thing I have discovered is that we will never stop doing it, so that is not an option. However, I have also discovered an approach to deal with this problem that is generally more successful than the terrible arguments we all experience.

I have observed and learned that if a double message tone is received, it most likely has been delivered. Therefore, we can adopt the assumption that if we are told we are giving a double message through our tone, it is most likely true. It may not be the message we want to give, and it may be mixed up with some other feelings of anger and frustration that have nothing to do with the situation. Whatever the reason, simply acknowledging this has very possibly happened can calm the moment and open the door for us to talk about what we are feeling. This discussion may not be very comfortable, but it is far more productive than the argument about whether it has happened or not. It also never hurts to apologize when we realize that we have really set a tone we didn't intend or one that created confusion and pain. This responsibility is not easy to assume, but it works.

The Blame Game

Blaming **is an ineffective form of communication.** We may all agree it is unproductive, but we also all use it to one degree or another. Its apparent ineffectiveness does not stop us from trying to use blaming as a way to communicate. Why is blame so ineffective? Why do we use it and how do we stop the *Blame Game*.

Blaming is ineffective because it is an attempt to communicate a feeling and thought we want the other person to understand, but in the process of blaming we fail to talk about ourselves and usually feel alone and defeated. We become a victim. Blaming ultimately gives away our personal power and sense of control, and we cannot solve stressful situations unless we have some personal power and influence over them and communicate that to others.

The feelings behind blaming are usually anger, hurt, or disappointment, and the blaming occurs when we began to tell the other person what he or she did to make the feelings occur. The blaming then degenerates into shaming and the other person then becomes defensive. The opportunity for understanding and even an apology are completely lost as the defending person counters by blaming the blamer. The *Blame Game* is well on its way to a full-scale argument.

Stopping the *Blame Game* involves the difficult and usually painful process of actually talking about our hurt, disappointment, and anger in a personal way that seeks to be understood. This means that I have to find a way to talk about me and how I feel and not to tell you about you and what you are doing wrong. My goal is to be understood and blaming provokes defensiveness and not understanding. Accomplishing the task of being understood empowers us and we are no longer victimized. When we can effectively communicate what we feel instead of blaming the other person, the game ends.

"Yesbut" the Word that Defeats Communication

Yesbut is not in the dictionary, but it should be. "Yes…but" is usually spoken so quickly it really sounds more like one word. *Yesbut* is a double message word that ends the giving and receiving of communication. *Yesbut* agrees and disagrees at the same time. It is a word that transforms a discussion into a circular argument. A *yesbut* in a marriage, family, business, church or any other organization can defeat any progress toward creating communication, relationship, solutions, and growth.

We have all been the *Yesbutter* at one time or another. So what makes us start using a word that is so unhelpful?

The answer is fear and anxiety. Whenever someone is presenting an idea or thought that makes us anxious or apprehensive we immediately seek a defense. For example, if I tend to be anxious about money, anything I hear that involves the expenditure or loss of money will likely illicit a feeling of anxiety. Since I may not want to appear cheap or uncaring, I might resort to the *yesbut* defense. "*Yesbut* we still owe $200.00 on the credit card."

Yesbut is the perfect defense because it agrees with the other person and defeats the idea or feeling that is making us anxious at the same time. The problem of course is that the other person then feels angry, misunderstood, and helpless, and the *Yesbutter* doesn't seem to understand why.

If you find yourself resorting to a *yesbut* defense, ask yourself what is making you anxious and try to understand it so you can listen. Wait to understand fully what the other person is feeling and saying before you attempt to talk about how you feel and what you think. "I like the idea of a new sofa and, of course, I get anxious about the $200.00 dollars we still owe on the credit card, so we need to talk and work it out."

Yesbut changing this defense is much easier said than done.

The Peril of "Fixing"

Whenever someone we love is in distress or has a problem, our natural inclination is to want to **fix it** for them. Our desire to make it better for another person is unquestionably a good intention, but trying to **fix it** for the other person carries a certain peril.

A Gary Larson cartoon depicts a dog leaning out of the car window bragging to his neighbor dog as he goes by, "I'm going to get tutored!" Like the canine victim of Larson's dark humor, the *fixer* is often very unpleasantly surprised that a good intention has such painful results. The reason for the painful result of trying to fix it is also contained in Larson's cartoon. It is no coincidence that neutering an animal is also referred to as *fixing.*

Whenever we *fix it* for another person, we take away that person's power to *fix it* themselves. We have *neutered* that person's empowerment to manage his or her own problem solving. A person usually does not receive the good-intentioned volunteer fixer in a positive way because most people really do want to do it themselves. This determination is so fervent that some people even refuse to manage a problem by paying someone like an electrician, plumber, or mechanic to *fix* the problem.

The defiant and determined toddler will give the message clearly as he or she pushes on the natural desire to be independent and successful. An even more defiant and determined teenager may deliver the same message to parents who are struggling to balance the desire for the teenager's independence and capacity for self-determination with the concern for safety, security and success.

As a spouse, parent, or friend, it is difficult for us to restrain our natural desire to *fix it* so that we can find a way to nurture and not neuter those we love. Sometimes the only thing we can say is, "I can see you are having a hard time. How can I help you?"

Why is it Always About You?

A young woman in her thirties recently discovered that she possibly had a heart problem and needed a series of tests to determine the nature of the problem. When she called her parents about the problem, her mother's first response was, "I hope it isn't serious. I couldn't possibly get down there for at least a few weeks. My schedule is just slammed." The young woman assured her mother that a visit would not be necessary and that she was confident it was not a serious problem.

Actually, the young woman was terrified she would need surgery, but she decided not to burden her mother with her feelings. She even felt guilty for bringing the subject up in the first place. Fortunately, she had a supportive husband and friends who would help with the children if necessary. She was not surprised about her mother's response and could not understand why it made her so sad. "I just don't know why it always has to be about her," she said.

I believe we can all be self-absorbed at times, but for some people it is a way of being almost all the time. Some people have great difficulty relating to the needs of others because, somehow, it is always about them. When that person is a parent, it can be very difficult for the children because they do not experience empathy and conclude that they must be doing something wrong. Children often fail to see that the self-absorption is the problem of the parent and not the failure of the child. Since the child of a self-absorbed parent becomes so adept at accommodating self-absorbed behavior, he or she may later marry a self-absorbed person. In the romantic phase of the relationship, the self-absorbed partner is overwhelmed with the attention and gratification he or she receives from such a "giving and loving person." Since the giving and loving person will inevitably fail to satisfy the needs of the self-absorbed person, the relationship will eventually suffer.

There are many varieties and levels of self-absorption. Often the person who is so self absorbed really doesn't want to be that way, but has found it to be the only way to cope with overwhelming anxiety or pain. The self-absorption can be a defense against feelings of inadequacy and shame. For the children of self-absorbed parents, healing begins when the child realizes he or she is not responsible for the parent's feelings.

In a marriage, it is important for both people to begin healing by understanding that neither the self-absorption nor the accommodation are effective ways of achieving a satisfying and enduring relationship. After achieving that understanding, the couple can begin the difficult but very rewarding journey toward a mutually satisfying and loving marriage.

"Kick *But*" and Improve Communication

The conjunction *"but"* may be one of the greatest deterrents known to effective communication. Whenever we attempt to communicate an idea to another person and we add to the idea by using the word "but," we essentially risk negating the first idea. "You did a good job, **but**..." No matter what is said next, the listener is prepared to hear a negative and probably has already forgotten the  first idea. "Your grades were really good this semester, but..." In the mind and heart of the listener the compliment has just been invalidated. "I love you, **but**..." Obviously this communication spells disaster.

It does not seem to be that difficult to *kick but* out of our conversations and either replace it with *and* or simply end the sentence to convey one idea at a time. However, it is a habit of communication that rarely leaves, even when we realize how destructive it can be. It takes practice and effort to really **KICK BUT.**

Creative Tension

When you say someone is *creative*, what do you mean? Creativity is considered to be something special that we attribute to talented and gifted people, but I think it is actually something available to all of us if we just grasp it. **Creativity is the ability to bridge the gap between vision and reality. It is the ability to *think outside the box*.**

The problem for most of us is that the gap between vision and reality is filled with tension. Creativity seems to always involve change and we are somehow constructed to be resistant to change. It is natural and very human to want safety, security, and a predictable world. Consequently we are always going to resist change. Creativity, therefore, inevitability involves overcoming our natural resistance and tolerating the tension to move into something new.

Relationship, marriage, parenting, and simply growing up and developing all involve our ability to use our natural tension and resistance as a path to change and to creativity. In fact it is often true that greater tension leads to greater results. Perhaps that is why we frequently marry people so different from ourselves. We often marry that which we want or envision for ourselves and then find ourselves in a tension we did not expect. Changing a vision into a reality means we must embrace tension and resistance as a bridge to the creation of what we want. **Creativity and tension are inseparable partners.**

Us

Romantic Love — Is it Real?

Valentine's Day arrives every year to celebrate romantic love. This kind of love has been the subject of literature and art since people could communicate with words and pictures, and it never loses its ability to *pique* the interests of humanity.

What is romantic love? Romantic love is union without boundaries and involves feeling perfectly understood and accepted, no matter what. Romantic love seems to permeate one's entire being with feelings of fulfillment and pleasure. The intensity of romantic love can trigger fear and awe that one can feel so passionately connected to another.

Part of the fascination with romantic love has to do with the fact that something we feel so intensely and passionately about is actually *temporary*. It comes and goes like the waves of the ocean and is gradually transformed in long-term relationships. Lamenting the temporal quality of romantic love, we often question whether it is even real.

Anyone who has experienced romantic love knows that the feeling is real. It is that intense intimacy between two people that involves allowing oneself to experience complete vulnerability, trust, and surrender. It is a mutual bonding that is emotional, spiritual and physical. It actually becomes the foundation of a union. Romantic love is an *idea* that marks the beginning of a joining together that must weather the numerous storms of life that challenge love. Using the tools of understanding, communication, patience and commitment, the love that begins as romantic love is gradually transformed by the winds and storms of life into a lasting love that is not an "ocean's edge" but the "ocean" itself.

Being *In Love* —
How Long Does it Last?

"It isn't like it was when we got married. I'm just not in love anymore."

"Where is the man I married twenty years ago? Where is the man I fell in love with?"

"I have changed and she has changed and I am just not in love anymore."

I have heard these words spoken many times because the idea of being *in love* is generally associated with the time at the beginning of a marriage when the relationship is fresh with romance and discovery. It is incredibly naive to assume that a relationship could be the same as it was twenty years ago. Therefore, what are people really talking about when they say they are just not in love anymore?

The best description of being in love came from a woman who reflected:

> *"When we got married I knew he was the person I wanted to spend the rest of my life with. Even at those times when I hated him I never thought of us as being apart. That was being in love, and the day I realized I couldn't imagine spending the rest of my life with him, I knew I was not in love anymore. It was horrible."*

Being in love is knowing that the presence of that other person is just the way life is supposed to be even when it is not fun and not happy. Being "in love" is essential for a successful marriage and it is challenged and threatened in many different ways over the years. When it is not there it is indeed a very serious problem.

How long does it last? Hopefully it lasts *until death do you part.*

58

Relationship Fitness

When couples arrive at my office, they are often in a relationship crisis. Usually two-way communication has stopped or regressed to contain only senders and no receivers. The atmosphere is generally unhappy, and each person is relating largely out of negative assumptions about the other. Both people have long since stopped learning new things about the other  and, therefore, neither one is feeling understood or important. It is a relationship crisis, and the couple may even be thinking about not being married anymore. It is a sad and scary time.

Marital therapy is designed to help couples move away from the negativity and reconnect their communication with and understanding of one another. Even when successful, this is an arduous process, and each couple seems to achieve it in a different way depending on the issues they are trying to sort out in their relationship. The time it takes to work through a crisis can vary from a period of a few months to over a year.

I think of a relationship as being a living, breathing, changing organism that constantly needs to be fed and exercised. Consequently, after the relationship crisis has passed, it is important for the couple work on *relationship fitness*. **Three parts of the *relationship body* need to be exercised.**

Appreciation
After the crisis it is important to not lose sight of what was almost lost. It is essential to not fall into the trap of taking each other for granted and forgetting to actively appreciate each other and what both contribute to the relationship.

Communication
There is one key to maintaining communication that will always work when communication threatens to break down. Plainly, that key is **listening. DO IT.**

Time

There are many distractions that keep us from spending quality time together. I think quality times are any occasions when we are clearly aware that we want to be with the other person and we feel the other person wants to be with us. Sometimes these occasions are spontaneous, but frequently they involve some planning.

A marital relationship is a very fragile being that can become weak and sick when it is not fed and exercised. Relationship fitness must be maintained for the entire life of the organism or it will die. A C T now if you think your relationship has grown weak and hungry.

Preventive Medicine for Marriage

I recently conducted a marriage enrichment seminar that was well attended by couples who were interested in strengthening their communications and relationships. As the day progressed it became increasingly clear that learning the intricacies of self-awareness, communication, and conflict resolution is not something most couples do, but something all couples struggle with daily. Trying new ways of relating is actually very hard work and also risky. The couples in the workshop were intrigued with the ways they would keep trying unsuccessful methods repeatedly without any awareness of the futility of their efforts. Most agreed that if their spouse would just change, it would all be better, and their effort was primarily to implement that change in their spouse. The resistance to this endeavor is enormous. It just does not work.

The preventive medicine for a marriage is actually to work on one's self. If we look at how hard it is to change ourselves, we can easily understand the impossibility of changing someone else. Looking in the mirror and seeing ourselves can be very difficult and sometimes painful, but it opens the door for change and is good medicine for our relationships.

Getting More Personal

Their marriage had become essentially a very negative experience with countless wounds, and yet they were determined to work on finding a way to stay married. It is an arduous task to work on a marriage when the walls have become so large and nearly impenetrable. Many are overwhelmed by the task and find divorce a better alternative; however, this couple pounded away at the wall until it began to break down. Their fear and resistance subsided and they decided to build on the present hoping it would help in healing the past. This decision was met with a mutual sigh of relief as they began to create a new *frame* for their relationship. They decided their immediate goal needed to be ***to get more personal***. They realized they really didn't know each other anymore and operated primarily out of negative assumptions without ever talking about themselves or their feelings. They looked at what they did to avoid being personal with each other and were very creative as they explored the defenses they used to keep each other at a distance. This work was very difficult but not nearly as exhausting and draining as the *war* had been. The frame they developed was important because it was hard for both to trust each other as they moved forward. The structure was a framework for a *new building*. One of the structures they created to enhance being more personal with one another was to have a discussion once a day that did not mention kids or money. They saw these topics as a way of distracting themselves from paying attention to one another.

Even in marriages that have not suffered a huge amount of negativity often suffer from the tendency to be less and less personal. The activities of daily living make it easy to pass one another without stopping and communicating. Perhaps it would be good for all of us to look at the things that distract us from getting more personal.

Unresolved Conflict

Does unresolved conflict lead to divorce?

Research shows that over half of what couples argue about is irresolvable! If you listen to couples' arguments as newlyweds and then again after they've been married for 25 years or more, you might be surprised to find that much of the content is the same. Too many people think that their marriages are in trouble because they continue to argue about the same things for years. But the truth is that this is very common. If you think that in good marriages people eventually find mutually satisfying solutions to all major problems, you've been fooling yourself. This is not what really happens.

Marriages and families are not ended because of differences. If this were the case, every marriage would end in divorce. Differences serve as easy explanations for why we can't stay married. The actual reasons people divorce are far more complex and can usually be discerned in how a couple deals with the irresolvable differences.

For many couples there is a mellowing and reluctant acceptance regarding unresolved differences. The arguments grow less heated and there is a mutual understanding that in spite of the differences this marriage is the place they want to be. Sometimes couples even learn to laugh about the irresolvable conflicts.

For many other couples there is not a mellowing but a growing anger and resentment that fuels the disagreements to become horribly ugly fights. These relationships are eventually filled with contempt and defensiveness.

The litmus test for successful marriage is not the unresolved differences, but the feelings of acceptance and understanding verses contempt and defensiveness.

Why Do Couples Fight to Be Right?

The "Fight to be Right" can begin with almost any comment, opinion, or observation. My experience is that the person who initiates the "fight" almost always does not intend to fight or even to be right. All the person wants is to express an observation, idea, or feeling. Although it usually occurs when there is a negative communication, it can also occur when the communication is positive.

She says, "I am glad we remembered your mother's birthday this year." He says, "I thought we always remembered her birthday." She says, "Yes, but we often get the card to her late." He says, "I don't think it is that often, and besides, she really doesn't mind if it is late." She says, "It is more often than I would like, and I feel bad if it is late." He says, "I just don't think we have forgotten that often. It is not a big deal." She says, "I think it is a big deal." He says, "It is not a big deal." She says, "Well, I felt bad when you forgot my birthday." He says, "I never forgot your birthday!" She says, "Yes you did. Three years ago." He says, "Three years ago! Three years ago? Really? "She says, "Yes, **really**!" He says, "I didn't forget. I was just a day late." She says, "Four days, actually." He says, "That can't be right. It was just a day late." (Etcetera, etcetera, etcetera)

This "Fight to be Right" could go on for paragraphs, and I am sure we could all write it, because I think we all do it, but **why?** Why do we engage in these futile "Fights to be Right," and usually forget why we were fighting in the first place?

I believe that it has absolutely nothing to do with being right. I think it has everything to do with a human need that is so deep and so important that it is far more painful than we realize when that need is not met. The need is the human craving to be "understood." There is probably nothing more gratifying than feeling understood, or more emotionally painful than not feeling understood. I believe this need resides at the core of our being. I think feeling understood emotionally, relationally, and spiritually is as important as the food we eat and the air we breathe. To be understood is to be emotionally embraced and nurtured. To be misunderstood is to feel rejected, alone, and even ashamed. This need is most important with the people we love, and therefore, the ones who can hurt us the most. We endure being misunderstood by the rest of the world all the time. I think that is why we are so sensitive to having that need met with our spouses, our parents, our children, our friends, our teachers, our pastors and all the people we allow to be close to our hearts.

A New Perspective: Whenever we are fighting to be right, it is probably because we are feeling the pain of not being understood. And, when someone we love is fighting to be right, he or she may be really struggling with that same pain. The essence of the message lies in the feelings and not in the words. You **hear** with your ears, but you **listen** with your heart.

Two Words That *Always* Confuse Communication and *Never* Help Resolve a Conflict

In an attempt to communicate a feeling, we often use a quantitative statement to communicate a qualitative issue.

> *"You are **always** late!"*
>
> *"You **never** help around the house!"*
>
> *"You are **always** complaining!"*
>
> *"You **never** let me do what I want to do."*

When someone tries to convey his or her dislike or disapproval related to something we have said or done, and the words "always" or "never" are in the description, we only hear those two words and miss the point. Interestingly enough, if someone says, "You are always nice to me," we immediately get the point even though we know we are not "always" nice. The difference is that the negative use of the words "always" and "never" results in feelings of hurt and defensiveness because we have been "unfairly" criticized. We are then determined to argue that the statement is simply NOT true.

Since I believe we will NEVER stop using quantitative words to validate our qualitative statements, it would be nice if we could ALWAYS be aware how ineffective these words can be in a conflict. It is much more effective to make a clear statement about how we feel.

"I get anxious and don't like it when you are late."

"I don't like it when you don't help around the house and I really like it when you do."

"I don't like it when you complain and have no solutions for your complaints."

"I wish you would help me do more that I want to do."

As you can see, these statements do not resolve a conflict, but they do introduce the issues so more discussion can occur related to the concerns in a framework that is not quantitative. They are statements about what you experience and how you feel. Hopefully they are not felt as criticisms that elicit defensiveness, but are experienced as invitations for conversation.

Togetherness and Separateness in Marriage

In an interview with Jimmy and Rosalyn Carter, Larry King commented on their long and successful marriage and wondered how they accounted for their achievement. Rosalyn responded with one word, *separateness*. She went on to explain how important it is for them to maintain their separate identities in order to enjoy their togetherness more fully.

Rosalyn's observation was quite astute because the balance of togetherness and separateness in a marriage is truly essential for a successful marriage. In marriage the paradox occurs that two *become one... and yet remain two*. Living in this paradox is not easy and the balance is something that needs to be negotiated constantly as the relationship, family, and careers constantly change.

When the togetherness is good and satisfying for both people, the separateness is experienced as affirming and energizing. When the togetherness is not fulfilling, the separateness can be experienced as abandonment or rejection. When there is not enough separateness or it is not satisfying, the togetherness can be experienced as consuming and even suffocating. Every marriage struggles to maintain the balance that is satisfying to both people, and it is often the source of conflict.

Maintaining the balance of togetherness and separateness is not a quantitative task. It is primarily a qualitative task. Separateness is improved by making the togetherness more fulfilling, and togetherness can be improved by valuing and encouraging the separateness that affirms individual identity. Accomplishing this balance of togetherness and separateness is a lifetime mission in a marriage.

Love Means *Always* Having to Say You're Sorry

The baby boomers remember Erich Segal's **Love Story** and the famous line from the movie in which Ali McGraw reassures Ryan O'Neal that "love means never having to say you're sorry." This refrain became the subject of many jokes in the early seventies. Certainly we baby boomers were seeking the meaning of love as I suppose every generation does in one way or another during those years of transition from childhood to adulthood. Love had been defined in thousands of ways over the centuries, but never like the character, Jenny (Ali McGraw), did in 1970.

Certainly we knew it then and we know it now. Love means *always* having to say you're sorry. There is no way to be in an intimate relationship and not hurt and disappoint one another. However, apologizing or saying, "I'm sorry," seems to be challenging in many relationships. Perhaps it is because we were forced as children to apologize as a way of shaming us for our misdeeds, but for whatever reason, the act of apologizing seems to be solely a confession of guilt in the minds of many people. Therefore, to say, "I'm sorry" is to say, "I'm wrong, guilty, and bad." If this is how it is perceived, no wonder it is so difficult.

We do and say things on countless occasions that hurt the people we love. Whether it is intentional or not, saying "I'm sorry" is purely the act of taking responsibility for our actions and letting the other person know we understand that we have hurt them. It is not easy because we do risk being shamed and blamed, and yet I have rarely seen this happen when a sincere apology is given that reflects an understanding of how the other person feels. If saying, "I'm sorry" is difficult for you, perhaps it would be good to rethink how you feel about apologizing. Conceivably you could begin to think of an apology as not being a confession of guilt and blame, but instead a mature act of understanding and empathy.

What Do You Assume About Your Mate?

When we first meet and during our courtship we have very few assumptions about one another. We are on a very steep learning curve about the other person and they are equally interested in learning about us. The experience of having someone who is interested in us contributes significantly to the feeling of *being in love*. However, as we learn more and more we begin to assume certain things based on prior knowledge and the learning curve begins to even out as romantic love is slowly and hopefully replaced by *real love*.

Getting married and making a life together is messy. A home is established, children are born, careers are built, and many assumptions are created. After about five years we are relating to one another almost entirely out of our assumptions even though our lives are changing and we are changing with each new day. The learning curve is nearly flat. This sounds rather grim but it is not so if we are primarily relating out of our positive assumptions.

- When you walk in the door of your home do you assume that your mate will be glad to see you? Do you anticipate a friendly greeting and a smile?

- When you approach your mate with a concern do you assume he or she will attempt to understand?

- Do you assume your mate loves you and has your best interests in mind even when he or she is angry with you?

If you can generally answer in the affirmative to these questions, then you and your mate have created a **relational sanctuary** that can deal with most any problem in this messy world. If not, you need to look seriously at your assumptions and how you can form new ones. However you answered, it is always good to keep that learning curve as steep as possible.

Becoming Aware

Sometimes the most simple observation reflects a profound insight. I experienced this a few years ago when I heard a frustrated husband reflect that it seemed every time his wife got angry, he got guilty. The result was that he thought her anger meant he had done something wrong, and he needed to do something to make her anger go away. He reflected that this certainly came from his childhood where he learned to take responsibility for everyone's feelings, especially his mother's. Consequently his wife usually felt she was not heard and often encountered her husband's defensiveness whenever she expressed a negative feeling. His awareness of this process enabled him to begin to be more open to listening and then responding.

Both husbands and wives often respond to one another out of what they have learned from the past and therefore don't really pay attention to the present. This can come from childhood or from years of habit in a marriage. The first step to changing it is to be aware of it. Each of us have many feelings that are connected to numerous past events that rest somewhere beyond our awareness. Gaining access to that particular *data bank* can be very liberating.

Seven-Year Itch

In the 1955 movie, "The Seven Year Itch," we remember the classic shot of Marilyn Monroe's dress blowing up around her legs as she stands over a subway grating on Manhattan's Lexington Avenue at 52nd Street. The movie was a comedy, but the reality of the seven year itch is not so funny.

The marital relationship goes through different developmental stages, beginning with what is known as the "honeymoon period." The period following the marital ceremony is marked by the continued enjoyment of each other's company and the desire to know and understand one another. However, the couple gradually grows into the routine of life together and begins to function and communicate more out of their individual assumptions rather than what each is learning about the other person. The couple settles into a rapport of daily living in which each begins to take the other for granted. This is not really a bad thing, but it is also not really a good thing.

The next stage is usually marked with the birth of a child. This represents a huge change, as the marital system becomes the family system. The rapport of daily living that was developed in the marital system is completely altered with the advent of the child. This is a time of major adjustment in which *both* the mother (wife) and father (husband) must bond with the new person in their life. A triangle of relationship is created, and the goal is for no one to be excluded. If this is accomplished, then all is well as the "seven year itch" approaches.

The **seven year itch** is actually that time when the couple begins to be aware of the many differences each experiences in their relationship and to find it more difficult to ignore the irritations and disenchantment each one experiences daily with the other. The tasks of building a family and/or career have been convenient distractions from the issue of how the couple deals with the disenchantment. For reasons I do not know, the seventh year seems to mark that time when the issue of disappointments is no longer ignored. Many couples make it past this time without significant problems, but many do not.

Our divorce rate is now fifty percent and rising. Many divorces occur between the seventh and tenth years of marriage. Established patterns of poor communication, negative assumptions and taking one another for granted all contribute to making a relationship tired and negative. The *seven year itch* begins as a painful passage, and it would be far better for many marriages if it could become a time of renewed interest and learning as the couple refocus on challenging their communication patterns and deal with the accumulation of disappointments that are nurturing a negative atmosphere.

The Thirty-year Hump

There are three *natural* events that can challenge or even traumatize a marriage. They are the arrival of children, the exodus of children, and retirement.

It is hard to believe such good things can also precipitate some very difficult challenges. I believe that the core reason for the difficulty is that we don't anticipate just how much the identities of the individuals and the family system change with each of these events. The adjustment is often greater than we could ever have imagined.

The marital event that is getting a lot of attention now is being termed the *Thirty-year Hump*. Baby Boomers (those born between 1946 and 1964) are being challenged by the fact that **one Monday morning after breakfast he puts down the newspaper and he is not going anywhere.** I say *he* because currently the most common problem in retirement involves how *he* will adjust to his new identity and how *she* will adjust to him. There are many wonderful exceptions to this generality, but not enough to keep the divorce rate for thirty-year marriages from being news headlines for the next twenty years.

Dealing with the financial realities of retirement is difficult to achieve but easy to envision. Dealing with the identity changes can be difficult to achieve because they are difficult to envision. If, for you, retirement just means that you are not working, then you could be in trouble. Planning for retirement means creating a new identity in your life and your marriage. All the Baby Boomers need to ask if we have really planned for the huge adjustment to the new identity that we have worked so hard to achieve. Even more important, hopefully we will set a good example for the generations to come because they will face the same issues at the *Thirty-year Hump*.

Marital Cancer

According to Peggy Vaughan, author of "The Monogamy Myth," first published in 1989 by Newmarket Press (third edition published 2003), very conservative estimates are that 25 percent of men and 15 percent of women will have an extramarital affair. These figures are even more significant when we consider the total number of marriages involved, since it's unlikely that all the men and women having affairs happen to be married to each other. In this case, it can be estimated that nearly 40 percent of marriages will be affected by an extramarital affair. These statistics are disturbing and even more distressing when one considers what it takes to recover when a marriage has to deal with an affair.

A marital affair is to a marriage what cancer is to an individual. No matter the outcome, people who survive cancer remember the rest of their life that they had cancer. They remember the horror, the anguish, the rage, the sadness, the depression, the hopelessness and the unrelenting fight to survive. This is all true even if their life becomes better than it was before cancer. A marriage survives an affair in much the same way. Like cancer survivors, affair survivors are faced with the same feelings and have to fight relentlessly and long to survive.

Fighting the "cancer" that can kill a marriage is hard and long. This must always be understood in order for both parties to join the fight together. One is usually devastated beyond belief, and the other, who had the affair, has to understand and commit to the healing process that is the most grueling and painful in the first year of recovery. Healing occurs as the pain is shared and the relationship is rebuilt.

I have seen many couples fight and win the war against *marital cancer* and I have seen many casualties. It is a lethal form of *cancer* that is fought by both people using the "medicines" of understanding, communicating, truth, patience, and an unrelenting commitment to survive and grow.

John Gottman's "The Four Horsemen of the Apocalypse of Marriage"

"Wives who make sour facial expressions when their husbands talk are likely to be separated within four years." John Gottman, Ph.D.

Why Marriages Succeed or Fail...And How You Can Make Yours Last, by John Gottman, Ph.D., is the result of over twenty years of scientific research with hundreds of couples. His observations confront us with many of the attitudes that are often overlooked but can lead to the end of a marriage. As the result of his research, he concluded there are four predictors of the deterioration and eventual end of the marital relationship. He calls these attitudes the *Four Horsemen of the Apocalypse: Warning Signs.*

First Horseman: Criticism

Criticism is contrasted with complaining. Criticism attacks the personality and character of the other person, whereas complaining involves specific behaviors. Criticism often begins with "You always...," "You never...," and "You are..." Complaining, on the other hand, is healthy and actually makes a marriage stronger.

Second Horseman: Contempt

Contempt goes another step beyond criticism and involves the "intention to insult and psychologically abuse your partner." The message to the partner is that they are stupid, disgusting, incompetent, and a fool. A mix of self-righteousness and shame are the weapons of contempt.

Third Horseman: Defensiveness

The response of defensiveness creates a victim who continually attempts to protect no matter what is intended. Defensiveness leads to denying responsibility even if there is a complaint. Excuses, negative mind reading, and whining are some of the weapons of defensiveness.

Fourth Horseman: Stonewalling

When one partner removes himself or herself from the emotional or physical presence of the other, a stone wall is created. The powerful weapons of the *stonewaller* are stony silence, disapproval, icy distance, and even smugness. Men seem to be the expert *stonewallers.*

These Four Horsemen seem to enter all marriages at different times. These are often the times of transition or loss. We should not underestimate their power to destroy. Also, we all can get John's book.!

The "D" Word

When couples fight, their conflict can become very heated. Tempers flare and words are used as weapons to disable and defeat one another. Sometimes fighting can become so desperate a couple will stoop to name calling as a way to disarm each other. When fighting gets to this point, they are in danger that someone will actually use the *D word.*

Of course the *D word* is **DIVORCE** and using it can escalate an argument or fight to a disastrous level. Using the *D word* introduces the end of the relationship and usually annihilates the opponent or escalates the fight to catastrophic proportions. **I refer to the *D word* as a *Dirty Bomb* that can do enormous damage when it is used in a fight.**

The commitment we know as marriage serves as a container for all our experiences and feelings in our relationship - the most wonderful and the most awful. As a *container,* marriage is a safe place to deal with the turmoil of surviving and growing in a chaotic world. It is the place where we experience the best and worst of the person we married, and sometimes we think about not being married. However, using the *D word* during a fight threatens to destroy the container and the safety it provides.

Divorce is extremely serious business and should only be discussed when it actually is a possibility. It should not be used as a weapon in an argument because everyone loses when the *D word* is unleashed and nothing is resolved.

The Sandwich Generation

Thirty years ago, gerontologists were referring to the *Baby Boomers* as the *Sandwich Generation*. They predicted that increasing life expectancy would produce a large population of elderly. Then the population of middle-aged Boomers would find themselves caring for teenage or young adult children and also caring for aging parents.

The prediction has come true as more and more of the middle age Baby Boomers become responsible for both their kids and their parents. At the beginning of this phase, the support of having helpful and nurturing parents and grandparents is a wonderful plus.

As the Boomers move into their fifties and sixties their parents move into their eighties and nineties; then parents begin to need more help to face the limitations of old age.

Serious illness and/or the loss of physical mobility mark the beginning of care giving needs most of us do not anticipate. In most cases, a family member, usually a daughter, steps in temporarily. Care giving soon becomes more than part time; more burdensome when spouses and siblings question decisions. The care giver's fatigue and resentment can be accompanied by a lack of knowledge which leads to impulsive decisions that create even bigger problems.

Here are a few suggestions for dealing with some of the challenges of the Sandwich Generation.

Denial can be a real enemy causing us to ignore signs of problems to come. Talk openly with your parents and encourage them to make plans. Get help if you can't talk to them.

Get on the Internet and research the health care and other resources available to your parent. If they live far away, don't move them close to you without great planning, thought, and discussion.

Make sure you have the information, authority, and documentation to direct your parents' care and mange their affairs if they become incapacitated.

Be empathic. Learn about grieving and loss. You, your family, and your parents will travel that road.

Life in the Sandwich carries many problems and also many benefits. Hopefully we can deal effectively with the problems so we can maximize the benefits of having parents with us a longer time than the previous generation could enjoy.

Sometimes On the Way to Heaven "All Hell Breaks Loose"

On June 29, 2008 I wrote the following.

I am sitting by my ninety-year-old mother's bed in the nursing home. It appears she is very close to dying. At least, that is the "clinical" picture today. It has been a path of steady decline over the last year, and she has maintained a strong positive determination to live. She is not very responsive today, so I am waiting and reflecting. Having worked in geriatrics for almost fifteen years early in my career, I have accompanied many families down this path. Of course, it is always different when it is "your" family and "your" path.

Death has a way of bringing families together and that can be both a blessing and a curse. Everyone arrives with their "baggage" that includes many memories, agendas, and unfinished business. It seems that the exhausting process of caring and grieving has a way of "loosening the latches on the baggage."

Mom died on July 1, 2008, and I have done a lot more reflecting since then. In my family the "unfinished business" and the "elephants in the room" all played a part as we were brought together around her last year of life when hard decisions had to be made and implemented. With the stress and the grieving, feelings became more intense as new and old wounds surfaced and resentments were fueled. A few times irritations and displeasures emerged and "hell" did break loose in its own "heavenly" way.

For me depression and anxiety became familiar companions. Knowing that this is a part of the process did not make it go away, but it did help knowing that something that felt so abnormal was really quite normal. This process is painfully familiar for many families when someone is "on their way to heaven." It was also helpful to know that something that seemed endless would end. The grieving would not end, but we worked to close our "baggage" after removing some of it and moving some of it around. The "elephants" are much harder to re-cover. My

therapist helped me a lot with that last task before he retired. I suppose we each have our particular tasks when death touches our lives, and sometimes "all hell" does break loose, and it hurts. Hopefully, we can find more healing as we deal with the hurt. It works better if we can talk to people who care about us and can listen, not fix.

Sit Down! We Are Going to Have a Talk

As a parent, how many *conversations* **have you had with your child that seemed to go nowhere.** We don't understand why they do some of the things they do and we try to teach them the right and easiest ways we have learned over the years. However, they just don't seem to want to listen to us. Whenever we reach this point of exasperation, we often are heard to say, "You are going to sit down right now and we are going to have a talk!" This usually means we are going to talk, and they are going to look at us with a defiant, incredulous stare that means, "How long do I have to endure this lecture?"

Perhaps we need to change our approach when we are so determined to communicate and try something new. I would suggest the statement, "You are going to sit down right now and I am going to listen!" Often I think kids are very willing to talk if they know we want to listen. It means we must indeed want to listen, and make every effort to do it.

If we can listen, they will talk, and they have a great deal to say. **Just listen.**

Spoiling the Child

Parents want their children to learn responsibility, discipline and an appreciation for what they have. This is actually a life-long task because we all strive to be responsible, disciplined and thankful when faced daily with the temptation to be otherwise. The best we can hope for our children is that we help them establish a path that values these attributes and commits to a life that enjoys more success than failure as they strive to be responsible, disciplined and grateful.

It is commonly believed that if we give a child too much and indulge their desires, we will be *spoiling the child*, and he or she will not be responsible, disciplined and appreciative. However, I don't believe that a spoiled child is the result of being given too much or too little. I think it is actually the motivation behind the giving that results in the spoiling.

Pampering another person does not spoil them. On the contrary, we feel cared for and special when someone pampers and spoils us because that is not how we are generally treated in this world. However, if we continually indulge and pamper a child or anyone else in order to take care of our own feelings or needs, that person does not feel cared for and special. Instead, that person actually feels used and confused because the person thinks and is told that he or she should feel good and be grateful.

If I give my child a beautiful expensive bicycle because I feel guilty that I don't spend enough time with her, then I am taking care of my feelings and not hers. If she senses my motivation, she will not feel loved and pampered. Instead, she will feel confused, used, sad and probably angry. If it happens often in our relationship, I will also be frustrated and confused and probably label her as being spoiled. She will say, "You just don't understand," and, ironically, she probably doesn't really understand it either. She just knows I think she is bad and ungrateful. She will also probably not be motivated to be responsible and disciplined.

Whenever we indulge a child to take care of our feelings, we are spoiling the child. As parents, we have all done it. If it has become a pattern, then we and our children have some work to do to get on a different path. This path is paved by understanding our motivations and dealing with our feelings and needs in a more open and effective way than indulging our child.

Ten Commandments for Divorcing Parents

I   You shall not assume that a divorce does not have a powerful effect on your child, no matter how young or old he or she may be.

II   You shall not assume that your child does not hear loud arguments no matter what time of night or day. If your child is in the house, he or she will hear you.

III You shall not make your child a confidant, and you shall clearly communicate that you understand your negative feelings about your spouse are your feelings and should not be your child's. You also shall not gain benefit from any negative feelings your child may have about his or her parent.

IV   You shall understand that your child will not betray his or her parent and suffers incredible pain when asked to take sides. Our children love us more than we can ever really appreciate and are heartbroken when forced to choose between us.

V   You shall not speak of your spouse or ex-spouse in a disparaging or derogatory manner in your child's presence, and you shall strive to overcome your own pain and/or anger in order to establish a civil rapport with your ex-spouse in the presence of your child.

VI   You shall maintain consistency of visitation and be open to accommodation for your child's needs whenever possible.

VII You shall be true to your word and keep your promises to your child in order to build and keep his or her trust.

VIII You shall not indulge your child to take care of your feelings of guilt. It does not work!

IX   You shall not use your child's feelings, time, problems, or any other needs to manipulate or punish his or her other parent.

X   You shall take responsibility to seek forgiveness and/or restore healing whenever you break a commandment.

The First Step for Stepfamilies

Stepfamilies are quickly becoming a very common form of family structure. Approximately 60% of all first marriages end in divorce, and about 75% of those who divorce will remarry. This year nearly 40% of all children will live with a stepparent.

The most common mistake stepfamilies, and some therapists, make is to compare the biological family model to the stepfamily model. A biological family is created when two people marry and have a period of time to enjoy the initial excitement of marriage and began to deal with their differences and disappointments. This is not an easy process, as the statistics attest. The marital couple begins to  develop a history together as they grow and create more and more memories. The *biological family* is then created with the arrival of a child and a new family history is added to the couple's history. The life cycle stages continue as the individuals and family unit change and grow.

The stepfamily model begins as a result of the interruption of the life cycle of the biological family. Therefore, it is important to understand that the stepfamily model represents a "new road" that branches off the previous road. The previous road cannot be traveled again. A new road must be constructed with its own particular feelings and experiences. **The fantasy that one can create a biological family experience in a stepfamily model is not helpful**. Giving up this fantasy is the first step toward paving the way for a new road, which can also lead to a fulfilling and happy family. The new road is not easy, but few roads through life are easily traveled. Understanding the particular stages of development the stepfamily undergoes is a way to get on the right road.

Blending Families

Blended family is another name for stepfamily. This term has been used more recently because it is more descriptive of how the mixing of different biological families occurs. There is a "blending" of histories, experiences, and relationships from the biological families of origin to form a new family unit. In the blending of families, there are tasks and issues that need to be recognized which are not found in the biological model of family life.

To form the blended family, the first task is to identify the groups being blended. A group is best defined as any two or more people who call themselves "we." The first "we" to be considered is the couple, because the couple must function as the hub of the new family circle and must guide the way as the family evolves. The other "we" groups include:

1. The children/child of each biological parent.
2. The children/child of each non-biological stepparent.
3. All the children living in the home with the couple.
4. The biological parent(s) outside the home and their biological children.
5. "We" subgroups also form among the children who are blended together from different biological families based on gender, age and compatibility.
6. Extended family, including grandparents, aunts, uncles and cousins, add to the "exponential" increase of "we" groups in the blended family.

Compared to the single biological family structure, the blended family is vastly more complex. This complexity can be so overwhelming some couples ignore it and hope everyone will adjust. This is not wise. To prevent a calamity, it is much better for the couple to meet the challenge directly by developing a Family Plan before the marriage or as soon as possible after the marriage.

Since each situation is so different, it is important to realize that each blended family needs a specific plan. As the couple takes the leadership to facilitate how the family will develop, there are three areas or categories to address. They are: Relational, Emotional, and

Practical.

The relational area involves identifying the "we" groups that will be affected by the change. For example, a son may have a strong relationship with his biological parents. He may perceive the arrival of a  stepmother as a threat to his relationship with his mother and his father. That perception needs to be taken seriously and addressed openly. Making a list or chart of the "we" groups can be very helpful when addressing the next area.

The emotional reactions of each group need to be identified. For example, an important emotional issue for the children is the grieving which naturally occurs as their world changes. Dealing with the losses openly can be much more productive than the common response of acting out the pain in anger and defiance. For example, the son who perceives the threat of a new stepmother may act out in fear and anger. In response, the couple leading the change can also become confused and frustrated. It is important for the couple not to respond with anger. This communicates rejection and that only confirms the threat. Feelings of hurt, sadness and fear are healed with open communication, understanding, acceptance and time. It is most important to ask the right questions that explore each person's feelings and experience as the family evolves. Using the chart or list of "we" groups, emotional reactions can sometimes be anticipated and addressed before they become serious problems.

The practical area of blending families is most difficult when the other areas are not addressed. Although it may be good for all families, it is actually essential in a blended family to deal with practical issues utilizing ample communication. I recommend regular family meetings to discuss schedules, plans and concerns. The meeting itself communicates the intent to build a family and the importance of each member.

Successfully blending families requires creating a structure that nurtures communication, openness, acceptance and inclusion.

Family Values:
A Counselor's Perspective

The other day I noticed a bumper sticker that said, "Hate is **NOT** a Family Value." I am not sure why that person had a truism for a bumper sticker, but it did stimulate me to think about the idea of "Family Values."

"Family Values" is a term that has been tossed around a lot recently, and I am not sure what it means because there must be hundreds of different family values in our western culture alone. Certainly most of us would agree that families have value, but it seems the values that are reflected in many families are very different. Perhaps that is why people are talking about it more and would like some sort consensus about what constitutes "good" family values.

As a Pastoral Counselor and Marriage and Family Therapist, I have a few ideas about some values that seem to help families function more effectively. I have noticed that families work better if they value communication, which actually means they value **listening**. This also means they communicate not only what they **do** but also how they **feel**. Feelings are not equated with behaviors but are understood as simply being true. We use feelings to inform the decisions we make about our behaviors, and parents who model making good behavior decisions have less problem guiding their children to do the same.

Along with the value placed on communication in an effectively functioning family, there is also an important value placed on respect. This does not only mean that children just respect their parents. Instead, there is an atmosphere of respect that tries to maintain the idea that "I am important AND you are important" even when we are frustrated or angry at each other. This can very hard to do, but families who strive to keep this value seem to be happier and have fewer problems making and keeping the boundaries and rules that enable them to function on a day-to-day basis.

Another value that seems to be important in an effective family is the value that is placed on individuality. This one is tricky because families are usually one unit under one roof, but each person under the roof is different. Each person has different needs, feelings, talents and personality. Daily living and functioning combined with preserving individuality in a family is not easy. I suggest that we strive to place a high value on being interested in each other and maintain a posture of always wanting to learn something new. Feeling accepted and understood in spite of our differences is a huge motivator for cooperating and meeting the challenges of living under the same roof.

Religion, sociology, anthropology and even government have many more important values to consider that would never fit on a bumper sticker, and are vital for creating and maintaining happy families. These are just a few I see from the perspective of many years of counseling and learning from individuals, couples and families.

When Trust is Lost

I believe that marriage is a **garden** we create when we exchange our vows. At that time we build a fence around a large garden (relationship) and inside this fence we plant other gardens. We grow flower gardens that reflect the experiences of joy, beauty and companionship. Some of the flowers are annuals and others are perennials we plant as we begin to establish our routines and traditions. We plant vegetable gardens that symbolize those things that nourish our relationship, such as our home, belongings and careers. The most important plant in the garden is placed in the center of the garden. It is an oak tree that represents our commitment and is nourished by love and trust. This oak is the most important plant in our garden and when it is damaged in any way, the marriage itself is endangered. The other plants can be neglected and even lost, but they can be restored with some attention and work.

When trust is lost or damaged, it is very difficult to restore. It is interesting that when one spouse loses trust, the other often has difficulty understanding how much damage has been done to the oak. Even when the oak has been severely injured by unfaithfulness, the unfaithful person frequently cannot understand why their spouse cannot recover more quickly.

When trust is lost, the one who loses it feels horribly betrayed, empty and hopeless. The whole garden suffers because the person who is betrayed no longer knows what is real and what to believe. The whole garden can seem like a mirage that has disappeared and is replaced by an arid desert. The terrible aloneness, isolation and fear that follow are devastating. The oak is poisoned and could die. If the oak dies, the garden soon becomes barren and the marriage is lost.

When trust is lost, every other aspect of the relationship that requires trust is questioned. If the spouse is late, doesn't call, goes on a business trip, stays on the computer, answers the Blackberry or is just quiet and preoccupied, the conclusion can easily be that something is wrong. When trust is lost, the wound is so great almost anything can stimulate the pain and doubt.

When trust is lost, the recovery of the oak depends on the determination of both people to understand the extent of the damage and to be committed to withstanding the storms of pain and grieving that follow. The oak must be fed with large amounts of communication, compassion, acceptance and patience. It takes an abundance of nourishment to overcome the hopelessness and restore the oak. Ironically, the restored oak is actually stronger than the original because the roots had to push deeper and the limbs grow thicker to withstand the storm when trust was lost.

Re-framing a Relationship

I have noticed that often we spend more time framing a picture then we actually spend on purchasing the picture itself. We see a picture or painting we like. Our feelings tell us almost instantly what we love it, and we buy it. The matting and framing of a picture or painting can make a huge difference in how the art is seen and experienced. A relationship can be like a picture we love. We can call it a "relationship picture," and it also has a frame that is vitally important because the frame of a" relationship picture" greatly influences how the "picture" is experienced.

In the beginning, a relationship is framed in trust, caring, love and friendship. In this framework, even the pictures of hardship and challenge are seen and experienced as "the good times." Often I have heard couples remark that it seems like they were much happier when they were struggling and had less than they are now when they have so much more. The "frame" of their relationship in the past was much different. They were a team who supported one another and communicated their love for each other.

As time passes the frame can become worn and weathered by differences, indifferences, disappointments, responsibilities and misunderstanding. As the frame changes, it is amazing how significantly the picture also changes. The feelings contained in the frame may become hostile, critical and uncaring. Consequently, even if this relational picture is placed in a large beautiful home that reflects wealth and success, the damaged and discolored frame creates a damaged and spoiled picture. To restore the picture, one must first restore the frame.

Once a couple realizes that it is the frame that needs to be changed, they can then take their individual responsibility to "reframe" the relationship. Reframing has to be done with both people working to challenge painful assumptions and memories that are destroying the frame. It is a difficult process because the tendency is to fall back into the old frame and avoid the risk and the vulnerability we feel in a more positive and trusting framework. Each one must exercise compassion and understanding for the pain the other experiences. Forgiveness has to become a "two way street" as each one can feel the other reaching out. Reframing a relationship requires very hard work that can be incredibly rewarding as a new and even more beautiful picture is created because the frame has been restored and sometimes even replaced. This is frequently the hard work of marital therapy.

Life

Which Land is Your Land?

Land of the "Has-Been"

The land of the Has-Been is a place where all our memories reside. It is a land filled with many high mountains, deep canyons, turbulent and still waters, blue skies and terrible storms.

Land of the "Should-Be"

The land of the Should-Be is hazy and foggy filled with mirages that come and go. It is a land created out of wants, needs, expectations, anxieties and hopes. It can be a land of liberation or a land of imprisonment.

Land of the "What-Is"

The land of the What-Is unfolds with every blink of the eye, every breath we take and every sound we hear. It is a real place that is constantly influenced and created by our perceptions, feelings and actions.

For human beings the land of the What-Is is the most difficult place to live because it is constantly informed and often deformed by the lands of the Has-Been, and Should-Be.

Sometimes we can't find our way out of the land of the Has-Been because we get stuck there with lost dreams, relationships, disappointments and painful memories. We may also get stuck there with wonderful memories we refuse to leave behind to face the more demanding or less happy land of What-Is. The land of the Has-Been always exists and should not be ignored. It should be visited to help inform the choices and assumptions we make in the land of the What-Is. It is the place we go, whether we like it or not, when we choose a mate, a career and how to relate to those in the land of the What-Is. It is a land to know and respect, but not a place to live.

The land of the Should-Be is often created out of our reaction to the land of the Has-Been. "I won't raise my children like I was raised." "When I get married it is going to be forever." The land of the Should-Be is enormous, filled with our ideas, hopes and aspirations to make our lives happier and better. It is important that it is our land of the Should-Be and not someone else's. It is a good land to visit and keep in our sights, but living there may confine us from the land of the What –Is.

Living in the land of the What-Is demands a constant awareness and balancing of the lands of the Has-Been and Should-Be. The balance helps us to make the best decisions and see our world clearly in times of light and darkness. Which land is your land at this moment? Is it where you want to be?

Failure, Rejection, and Hope

An old friend and colleague, whom I had not seen or spoken to for many years, recently found me on the Internet and sent me an email. As we proceeded to bring each other up to date on our lives, Allen wrote that over the years his life has endured many changes, and he has come to realize that the best changes in his life have been introduced by rejection and failure. Consequently he hoped to encounter many more rejections and failures in the next twenty years of his career.

Allen offered a rather interesting twist on something that most of us spend a lifetime trying to avoid. Rejection and failure are so painful we certainly do not identify them as the indication of good things to come. However, Allen is really quite correct in his observation. As one looks back on life's journey the crossroads that have led to success, happiness, and fulfillment have often had their beginning in an experience of rejection and failure.

It is true that the idea that out of brokenness comes wholeness is at the core of Christian theology and it represents the mission of Christian ministry. Allen's hope to encounter many rejections and failures is an intriguing statement of faith.

The Illusion of Control

I have often said that God instilled the idea of control in our minds as a kind of sick joke, and whenever we imagine we are in control of our lives, God laughs. I don't really believe God practices sick humor, but it is very frustrating sometimes to persist being in control when it is a never-ending battle. It seems that every time we think we are "in control" we are reminded that we are not. However, we have been created to hold on to the *illusion of control*, so we just keep struggling. So what is this about?

I believe the illusion of control is another one of those very difficult paradoxes we struggle to manage throughout our lives. No matter what we are doing we are always struggling to control. Think of each day growing up, going to school, getting a job, losing a job, getting married, staying married, raising children, growing older, losing loved ones, getting sick, getting well, and finally dying. Throughout our lives we wrestle to be in command of our lives, and we are brought to our knees each time we think we have succeeded.

I believe a friend of mine, who was dying of cancer, had the answer to the paradox. He told me that he had finally realized that the only reality he could actually control was the present. "The past is now a memory and the future is not in my hands. The present moment is the only reality that is truly in my grasp," he said. This certainly did not mean that he stopped fighting to take command. He fought till his last breath. It did mean, however, that the quality of his life greatly improved when he really appreciated the control he had in the present. I think our capacity to remember the past and envision the future gives us an illusion that causes us to forget our limits and not appreciate what we really can control. What do you do with your moments in the present? Do you really appreciate what you have in those moments, or are you too busy with the illusions?

Letting Go of Hurt

Letting go of hurt can be one of the most difficult tasks in a relationship. Sometimes the hurt is so painful we find ourselves unable to let go of it. At those times the hurt can begin to become like a cancer that spreads through the relationship slowly and insidiously killing it. This is not what we want but we feel helpless to stop it. We become entrenched in blame and anger, and the environment for the *cancer* to grow is ideal.

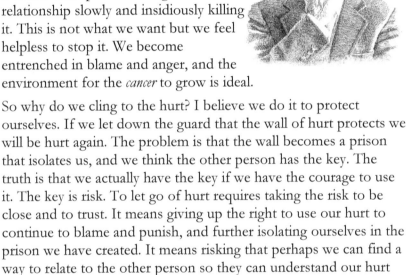

So why do we cling to the hurt? I believe we do it to protect ourselves. If we let down the guard that the wall of hurt protects we will be hurt again. The problem is that the wall becomes a prison that isolates us, and we think the other person has the key. The truth is that we actually have the key if we have the courage to use it. The key is risk. To let go of hurt requires taking the risk to be close and to trust. It means giving up the right to use our hurt to continue to blame and punish, and further isolating ourselves in the prison we have created. It means risking that perhaps we can find a way to relate to the other person so they can understand our hurt without feeling blamed or punished. Usually relating out of our hurt has become so habitual that we have to work hard to achieve the kind of vulnerability required to let go. It can take a long time.

Letting go of our hurt and continuing a relationship requires that the other person must achieve a posture of understanding and a willingness to listen. When someone releases them self from the prison of their hurt, it is important he or she is received and understood. Letting go of hurt is a two-way street that must be traveled by both people if a relationship is to be healed.

If the relationship is irrevocably broken, we are challenged to grow self-love, self-assurance, and self-confidence – the keys that unlock the doors to our prison. We must attempt being loved again as opposed to containing ourselves safely behind the walls of our fear and bitterness.

Live Into It

Her husband had decided to proceed with the divorce. She was struggling to know what her new situation was going to be like. She was entering a world that was unknown and full of some dreadful possibilities. As she struggled with her dilemma, she tried to think of all the possibilities, all the problems, and all the solutions. She was overwhelmed. Finally she sat back, stared ahead into space, and with a sigh she declared, "I will just have to live... into it."

There are moments in life when the road turns in a completely new direction. It is a direction that is totally unexpected and usually terrifying. At that time it is hard to describe what is happening to us and yet we search for words that will somehow begin to contain the experience. We feel out of control and helpless and we intuitively know that if we find a way to talk about it, we can somehow take a step toward it and through it.

Times like these are shared by all of us, to one degree or another. Accidents, rejection, disease, death, divorce, and unemployment are times of transition that leave us suspended and paralyzed in life without anything or anyone to grasp upon.

Finding the words offers the beginning of a lifeline. For the woman facing divorce those words were, "I will just have to live... into it." With that resolve she had a moment of clarity in which she could finally step forward onto the road she had to travel. "Live into it," **is** something we all have to do at different times in our lives, and perhaps her words of faith and assertion can help us when we have to find words to form our own lifeline and go on down the road of uncertainty.

A New Year Re"soul"ution

*When you were born, you were crying
and everyone around you was smiling.
Live your life so that when you die,
you're the one who is smiling
and everyone around you is crying.*

Author Unknown

With the New Year comes promises to lose weight, pay off the credit cards, start exercising, spend more time at home, attend church more regularly, work harder, work less, spend less money, make more money, and reduce *stress*.

Needless to say, the resolve fades as life continues in much the same way it has year after year. Many people don't even make resolutions anymore, because the resolutions simply become measures for disappointment instead of success.

Perhaps it would be more useful to think about what we want to *be* rather than what we want to *do*.

Replace resolution with *re(soul)ution* and reflect on the condition of one's soul rather than the solution for one's condition.

Are you living life so that you are happy and smiling? Are you making a difference in the lives of those you love and those you live with in this world? What is your goal for living? If this is your last year, can you end it smiling and others crying?

Attitude of Ingratitude

I was driving in Atlanta rush hour traffic this morning and needed to change lanes because I was behind a slow moving truck. I had the choice of shoving my way in or signaling my need and hoping someone in the line of traffic would let me move into the lane. Since I generally signal and don't shove, I signaled for a left turn and waited. One car passed, but the next held back to let me change lanes. I waved to indicate my gratitude and he waved back. It was a simple moment, probably repeated thousands of times in Atlanta traffic this morning, and it occurred to me that people do generally want to do good things, and they also like to be acknowledged for their good deeds. It also occurred to me that people sometimes develop an attitude of ingratitude and take for granted the goodness of others. This attitude of ingratitude indicates a kind of self-absorption that results in a feeling of entitlement. Had I felt I was entitled to be in the other lane, I would have shoved my way in, but I don't think I was actually entitled to move over. Everyone on the road was trying to get where they needed to be, and my time was no more important than any other person's time. I decided the privilege to move over was a gift I could only hope someone would give, and I believe it was my responsibility to express my gratitude for this gift.

It is often said that we should not expect something in return for our acts of goodness or kindness. However, I believe we are disappointed when we are not acknowledged. I believe this is how we were created and there is nothing wrong with needing to be appreciated. On the other hand, **I believe there is something terribly wrong with the attitude of ingratitude, in which I would expect others to give and accommodate me without my appreciation.** This is a sad condition of self-absorption that we can all suffer if we take others for granted. Unfortunately, it happens often with the people we love the most, and it spreads into our daily routine where we begin to take the people, and even the gift of having a daily routine, for granted. Becoming self-absorbed can be easy and comfortable, but self-absorption is a very lonely place to be.

Everyone Suffers from Depression

It seems odd there is any stigma that accompanies the problem of depression when it far more common than the head cold or even allergy conditions. Unlike other ailments we contend with, we use all kinds of different ways of avoiding the word, depression.

> "I'm just in a bad mood."
> "You seem to have had a bad day."
> "Oh I was just down in the dumps."
> "I just feel tired all the time."
> "Can't seem to sleep lately."

All of these are descriptions of depression. Depression comes in many different forms and its intensity is often in direct proportion to the external or internal conflicts or stresses we are experiencing. The source of depression can be added pressure at work or home, or it can be as significant as the death of a loved one. It can also have its roots in a lifetime of living out early childhood dilemmas and messages from our family of origin. Whatever its origin, depression is as essential to our psychological well-being as pain is to our physical well-being. Depression, like physical pain, simply tells us something is wrong and we need to pay attention to it.

Part of the insidious nature of depression is its power to make us feel ashamed of being emotionally vulnerable. This is an irrational conclusion, because one who is not emotionally vulnerable is not human. It is how we are made, so we can relate to one another and not be alone. Like physical pain, depression is sometimes severe. However, even though we seem to have no problem seeking help from others for a serious wound or laceration, we are far less likely to even let people know of the deep psychological and emotional wounds we might suffer. Perhaps if we realize that everyone does suffer from depression, then maybe it will not be so hard to share it and let others understand, which ironically is also the best medicine for depression.

A "Cure" for Depression

Clinical depression is one of the most debilitating emotional and mental maladies that can occur in a person's life. However, most people are never subjected to this kind of paralyzing experience, which requires extensive medical and therapeutic treatment. Most of us experience a less toxic form of depression that can leave us helpless, confused, sad, angry, afraid, and unmotivated. Sometimes it comes with no apparent explanation, and other times it comes when life is particularly painful and difficult for clear and understandable reasons.

The path that takes us to the other side of depression is different for all of us and often depends on the situation we are dealing with in our lives. After walking this path with hundreds of people over many years, I have noticed there is one common remedy that people frequently use to get through a depression. **That *cure* involves simply making contact with another person.** We are most vulnerable to the demons of depression when we are alone with our own thoughts and feelings about our situation and ourselves. When we are alone fear, sadness, anger, anxiety, doubt, and helplessness are exceedingly skillful at tormenting us. Forcing ourselves to make contact with other people can greatly reduce the power of these demons of depression.

Relating to others as a way of dealing with our depression is a powerful tool to use along with other resources as we struggle with depression. There are many tools which work to varying degrees for different people. The power of relationship is a tool that we all rely on to help us through the bad times.

Revisiting Norman

Norman Vincent Peale wrote *The Power of Positive Thinking* in 1952. In the 1970's many considered this book, which mixed the idealism of religion and the science of psychology, to be a naïve, simplistic, and obsolete view of the world. Of course the fact that the book sold almost 20 million copies in 41 languages may have indicated that it had much more of a universal appeal and timelessness than was acknowledged.

The 1970's represented a time in our history when we struggled with a darkness that was not a force from the outside, but one that seemed to emerge and torment us from the inside. It left us with a population of people whose divorce rate has risen to 67%.

The latest studies reveal that the pervasive characteristic of the failing marriage is an atmosphere of negativity. Negativity is now seen as something which can insidiously infect people and destroy relationships.

Dr. Peale's teaching may have been interpreted in many different ways, but his ideas about the power of the positive certainly cannot be ignored when we are so painfully aware of the power of the negative. Positive thinking is not simple. It is not easy. It is not impossible. Perhaps it is time to pay Norman another visit and sift through his wisdom. **"Change your thoughts and you change your world."**

Grieving Heals

When you cry, have you ever noticed how your vision becomes so distorted as the tears form and then your vision becomes so clear the moment the tears begin to flow down your cheeks?

Recently, someone made this comment during a self-reflective moment regarding the many tears she had shed over the last few weeks. At first I didn't really get it, but, with some thought, I realized that indeed our vision is completely distorted when tears well up in our eyes, and the moment they begin to flow our vision actually becomes remarkably clear.

It is a good metaphor for how grieving works. The purpose of grieving is actually to help us adjust to loss and see the world around us with a new clarity and acceptance. Like the tears, we hold back the pain of grieving as much as we can, but when we let it flow, we understand with our heart and mind the truth of the loss we are experiencing. The biology of crying even reveals that tears contain proteins and hormones that are possibly *waste products* created by pain and stress that need to be released. There is something cleansing and healing about grieving both psychologically and biologically.

In whatever way one approaches the meaning of grieving, it seems that we are created to have this capacity to grieve so we can be close, love one another, and invest ourselves fully in relationships. With the God-given capacity to grieve, we can adapt to the inevitability of experiencing loss and therefore take the risk of being close. People who do not allow themselves to grieve can become severely depressed, isolated and relationally paralyzed. Grieving can take a long time when losses are great, so patience and understanding are very important as the tears and the grief flow.

Secret of Success

When people are blessed with great success they are often asked about what accounts for their achievements. Many will say that it is hard work, support from friends and family, endurance, and even luck. All of these contribute to success and are often essential to any accomplishment.

I believe that you will never achieve real success unless you like what you are doing. In fact your chances for success are directly proportional to the amount of pleasure you gain from what you do. Recently a friend, who has been immensely successful at her work, decided to quit. When asked why, she responded that she just wasn't having fun anymore. She went on to say, "I have always believed that if you have a job you don't like, face the fact honestly and get out. Work is reward, not punishment."

It is really quite simple. If you enjoy what you do, you'll be successful and if you don't enjoy what you do, you won't be successful. Your success in any occupation depends on your enjoyment and love for your work. Even on the bad days you know that you are doing what you like. Success in its highest form calls for peace of mind, enjoyment, and happiness. The secret of success is finding the work that you like best and not doing your best at work you like least.

You don't *pay* the price for success. You *enjoy* the price for success.

What if all the liquor stores were to announce that from now on all alcoholic beverages, with the exception of premium brands, would be available for the flat rate of $29.95 per month?

Of course this is a preposterous question, but that is precisely what has happened with pornography, another addictive substance.

Those of us in the psychotherapeutic world have known for many years that pornography can have powerful addictive properties. Like alcohol, it has been regulated by laws, cost and availability. Now pornography is available on the Internet in nearly unlimited quantities for a flat rate.

Although popularized in a television show many years ago to reflect a complex system to apprehend criminals, a dragnet is actually conical shaped fishnet that is dropped to great depths to catch fish. Internet pornography is like a dragnet in the depths of the Internet that catches thousands of people every day. Those of us in the field of psychotherapy, marriage counseling, and ministry have long been aware of the swelling problem as the *dragnet* has grown larger with increased internet use and speed. The number of referrals related to the addiction and the relationships it affects are increasing for all clinicians, even though most people have only a surface awareness of the problem as strange pop-ups and emails mysteriously appear on computer screens.

The Internet Dragnet has been largely ignored because it operates under the surface of public awareness and unlike alcohol addiction, the person who is addicted to pornography is the only one who knows and usually keeps the secret until it becomes completely unmanageable or is discovered.

The good news is that the addiction and the damaged relationships are treatable. The addict who is caught in the Dragnet is often relieved to find freedom. Counselors and many ministers can provide confidential guidance and resources for stopping the behavior. In addition, there can be intense feelings of anger and betrayal in a relationship that needs to be healed through support and counseling. Overcoming an addiction and its consequences requires commitment and hard work.

When All is Lost

I have been with many people as they suffered enormous losses, and recently I have experienced this kind of huge catastrophic loss with a very close friend. As I have seen the pain and agony of his grieving I have been called to wonder again how we search for meaning when all is lost.

Viktor E. Frankl was a professor of Neurology and Psychiatry in Vienna, Austria and the author of 32 books, including *Man's Search For Meaning*. Dr. Frankl was a survivor of four Nazi concentration camps, among them the most infamous, Auschwitz. His wife, father, mother, and brother all died in the camps; only he and his sister survived. In *Man's Search For Meaning*, Frankl did not consider himself a hero, rather he describes the heroes or *saints* to be among those in the camps who gave up their portions of bread to others, or gave their lives in order to save someone else from the gas chambers. He grasped the truth that the salvation of humanity is "through love and is love." He leaves the reader in awe of his determination to survive in the midst of horrendous carnage. Frankl uses words to portray haunting images in a masterpiece he wrote from the depth of his soul. He paints images, not of extraordinary human beings, but of extraordinary circumstances, which led average individuals to become in their own way, masterpieces of humanity.

Out of his experience with the worst that humanity could possibly endure he learned and concluded:

> *Everything can be taken from a man but...the last of the human freedoms - to choose one's attitude in any given set of circumstances, to choose one's own way.*

It's Not a Problem Unless...

Problems confront us every waking moment and sometimes even in our sleep. A *problem* is technically one of those moments when we have to make a choice and making choices start each day when we hear the alarm and have to decide when we are going to respond and get out of bed. After that initial step out of bed we are faced with hundreds of choices or *problems* throughout the day.

Developing routines help us greatly because the problems or choices are structured with solutions that were previously determined. Without routines and structures that automatically solve problems we can become overwhelmed and can feel helpless. Interrupting routines can be very frustrating particularly when the disruption creates the need for new solutions to attain our goal.

I have found it helpful to re-frame the way I think about problems and solutions. I try to always remember that, ***it is not a problem, unless there is a solution.*** Whenever the structures and routines of our life no longer automatically solve our problems, we can began to feel helpless and out of control. This is the time to consciously remember that there are always solutions to problems, even when we are overwhelmed and cannot immediately see the solutions. Overwhelming ourselves immediately paralyzes our problem solving ability.

Sometimes the solutions for very large problems are not clear. At these times a *problem* graduates to the level of a *dilemma* which means we must attack it with many different resources and struggle to not be defeated and to find the answers we need. These are the times we need to seek help, support, and effective guidance.

There are often many ways to solve a problem. Maintaining a focus on the solutions helps us sustain a positive attitude. Our mind-set toward our problems often determines whether our problems are solved or not.

I Am Entitled!

It is quite frustrating dealing with a person who suffers from the idea that, "I am entitled." When we have an attitude that reflects entitlement we usually communicate that we expect others to accommodate us without the even the simplest sincere acknowledgement expressed in two words like, "thank you." This represents a sad condition of self-absorption that we can all suffer if we take others for granted and do not convey our gratitude. Unfortunately, it happens sometimes with the people we care about and love, and it too often also spreads into our daily routine. Becoming self-absorbed can be easy and comfortable in a world filled with so many commitments and far more conveniences. Unfortunately, the people serving us can become objects that are just another one of the amenities we enjoy. Unhappily, self-absorption isolates us in a is a very lonely place that can become a "garden" that grows angry feelings of blaming and a lot of complaining. Ironically, self-absorbed people are the most offended when they are treated as they treat others.

It is not easy to maintain an "attitude of gratitude" in a world that is so stressful it draws us into a safe cloud of negativity that spoils the joy of connecting with others. However, when we do let ourselves experience real thankfulness and gratefulness for our many blessings, we feel connected and not so alone in this difficult and complex world. We say, "please and thank you" just as most of us were taught. It also really helps, and doesn't hurt in the least, to look into the eyes of the other person and smile! It makes the day better for both of you.

The Truth Will Set You Free.
But first it will make you miserable!

Epilogue

What has been will be again, what has been done will be done again; there is nothing new under the sun.
Ecclesiastes 1: 9

"Nothing is new under the sun" is a truth we often forget. I believe perceptual dissonance and perceptual synergy are not new ideas. They are simply new "frames" that might help us freshly ponder the "mystery" of human relationship and maybe do it a little more effectively. Perceptual dissonance and perceptual synergy offer an additional framework for the challenge of human relationship that prophets, philosophers, theologians, psychologists and scientists have struggled with for thousands of years. It is immortalized in the narrative of "Adam and Eve" as the first couple to suffer the pain of perceptual dissonance struggling with the battle between our heads and hearts. Each human is a unique combination of nature and nurture. Therefore, our perceptual worlds will always be different, and this difference really confounds ME, YOU, US and LIFE.

We live in a paradox where nothing is new, and everything is new. Our struggle to communicate and relate to one another as harmoniously as possible is not a new concept but a challenge we face every day. The frameworks of religion, philosophy, psychology and medicine all strive toward the goal of attaining a higher level of human understanding and achieve communicative relationships that transcend our primordial instincts of "fight or flight," and the instinctive attraction to the negative we were "hard wired" to pursue for protection and survival in the primeval world. Our technology and social media has raised our level of self-awareness and other-awareness to a global level that is taking us to something that is "new under the sun."

In 1991, the technology of video cameras made it possible for the world to witness Rodney King being beaten by the Los Angeles police. This resulted in the Los Angeles riots of 1992, and Rodney King's famous plea, *"People, I just want to say, can't we all get along? Can't we all get along?"* It was as if the world stood still for a moment and pondered the ideological question and the clarity of its resolution that was at the same time uncomplicated and paradoxically overwhelmingly difficult. Over twenty-five years later we are still embroiled in the anger, intolerance, hatred and violence perpetrated by so much perceptual dissonance between individuals, couples, communities and countries.

The framework of perceptual dissonance becoming perceptual synergy is one way to promote effective human communication and relationship. This begins with ME, YOU, and US becoming more reflective, insightful, vulnerable, empathic and finally truly understanding. It begins with LIFE not being something we do by taking one breath after another, but it is something we celebrate as a gift we are bestowed and should be cherished with loving stewardship. Perceptual dissonance is unpleasant and painful, but it is also the necessary opportunity to pursue perceptual synergy. The differences in our perceptions are always an invitation to listen, learn and connect in a spirit of understanding that transcends our differences and our disagreements. It is the beginning of the perceptual synergy that can generate a creativity that destroys the walls dividing YOU and ME, and it challenges US to leave our comfort zones of complaining and blaming and seek to listen, learn and understand one another enough to "get along AND get it done" so all of us can live LIFE fully.

W .ICE·gov Localb

A 21 30   65D

A 21 3023 650
Venezuela

CPSIA information can be obtained
at www.ICGtesting.com
Printed in the USA
FFHW02n0452200818
47780735-51473FF

9 780692 156230